Notes from Ramallah, 1939

Notes from Ramallah, 1939

By Nancy Parker McDowell

Foreword by Tony Bing

Friends United Press
Richmond, Indiana

This book is made possible in part by a grant from the Obadiah Brown Benevolent Fund/Sara Swift Fund, New England Yearly Meeting of Friends.

Book and cover design by Shari Pickett Veach
Back cover photo of Ramallah by Roger Hawley

Library of Congress Cataloging-in-Publication Data

McDowell, Nancy Parker, 1916-
    Notes from Ramallah, 1939 / by Nancy Parker McDowell ;
    foreword by Tony Bing.
      p. cm.
    ISBN 0-944350-59-3
      1. McDowell, Nancy Parker, 1916- —Diaries. 2. McDowell, Nancy
    Parker, 1916- —Journeys—Palestine. 3. Palestine—Description and
    travel. 4. Råm Allåh (West Bank)—Description and travel.
    5. Madåris a-Frindz (Råm Allåh) I. Title.

DS107.3 .M22 2002
915.694'044—dc21

                      2002021505

Contents

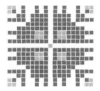

Foreword

The year 1939 was one of the defining years of the twentieth century. World War II broke out in Europe, and in the Middle East the Arab Revolt (1936-39) reached an uneasy conclusion with the signing of the British White Paper. The White Paper limited Jewish immigration and land purchase. Though the Revolt was officially ended, tensions among the British, Arabs, and Jews continued to mount, leading ultimately to the War of 1948.

Into this time of turbulence came a young American Quaker, Nancy Parker (later McDowell), who arrived in Palestine as a volunteer teacher at the Ramallah Friends Girls School. The narrative of her experience is an interesting window through which to view the struggle for Palestine and the fears about an impending war in Europe (as Nancy states: "There's something awful going on in Germany.").

Nancy Parker's correspondence and journal also give us a fascinating glimpse into one year of the hundred-year effort of Friends to sustain an educational mission among Palestinians. She writes and sketches simply and perceptively about the competing claims of Arab and Jew for Palestine, that at the time of her journey had produced a conflict of more than forty years. This conflict intensified during the oppressive presence of the British occupation during the Mandate Period (1922-1947).

There is, as well, a contemporary ring to her narrative. Anyone familiar with the last thirty-four years of Palestinian resistance to Israeli occupation will realize that Nancy Parker's 1938-39 accounts of collective punishment, administrative detention, house demolition, and suppression of guerilla movements might well describe life in Ramallah in the year 2002. Only the name of the oppressor (Israel for Great Britain) has changed. For instance, she describes one hundred and seventy houses demolished in one village as reprisal for a British death, and the collective punishment of cutting off of telephone and mail communications because Ramallah was rebel headquarters. The fact that resistance to foreign rule has been the staple for Palestinian life throughout this century, and indeed goes back into the Ottoman period, helps us understand better some of the political and cultural issues underlying the current conflict in the Middle East.

When Nancy Parker got off the boat in Haifa in September of 1938, she moved into a divided society, where one either went by Jewish bus along Jewish roads past Jewish villages, or by Arab bus along Arab roads past Arab villages. Where one was identified by wearing either a hat or a headdress, and where Americans were pressured into taking sides even though their deepest wish might be to be friends with all the inhabitants of the region.

Nancy's correspondence gives the reader an understanding of how Quakers have struggled to be a force for reconciliation and positive social change in times of great conflict in the Middle East. Nancy befriends a young Jew on his way to Palestine after fleeing European fascism, but she can't afford to sustain the friendship because of her teaching position in the Arab society. She deplores the violence that accompanies the British occupation in

Ramallah, yet serenades the British soldiers at Christmas and gets
a ride in their armored car to Haifa. Here is a clear view of a young
Quaker woman's optimism, spiritual grounding, compassion, and
anguish as she confronts the conflict and how her personal
experience parallels the experience of other Quaker volunteers at
the Ramallah Friends Schools during more than one hundred
years of Friends involvement in the Middle East.

Nancy Parker also conveys the beauty of the land and the warm
hospitality of its Arab inhabitants. Her sketch of Arab culture,
including the ritual gathering of spring wildflowers, the pressing
olives for oil, the threshing of grain, and the making of bread and
tabbouli has a timeless quality about it familiar to any traveler to
the region.

Few travelers are as intrepid, courageous, curious, and
adventuresome as our Miss Parker, who climbs the Pyramids, steps
out of her train in Luxor in her bathrobe, toothbrush in hand,
onto the royal carpet laid out for the visit of King Farouk's mother,
who leaps onto moving trains at the last minute, and who, with
her friend Gertrude, travels unprotected in Damascus, Baalbeck
and Amman (where she rides with Emir Abdullah in a bullet-
proof car). Her narrative also captures her lively presence at the
Friends Girls School, where she leads terrified girls across a
courtyard as British and Arab bullets whiz by her, and where she
directs the first dramatic production ever held at the Friends
schools and offers (albeit unwittingly) the first class in sex
education.

The reader of this small volume thus can approach the
narrative on many levels — as history, as culture, and as an
example of Quaker experience and concern — but above all, as a
portrait of a twenty-two-year-old whose love of life, adventure,
curiosity, humor, sense of the dramatic, and ability to flourish
under rough and dangerous conditions are revealed to us through

delightful prose and art. For those of us who know Nancy Parker McDowell's life for the sixty years that follow her safe return to the United States, we are struck by how the qualities revealed in this narrative are as freshly embodied in her now as they were in 1938-39.

Tony Bing
Executive Director of the Peace Studies Association
Director Emeritus of Peace and Global Studies, Earlham College

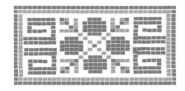

Introduction

In the fall of 1938 I was sent by the American Friends Service Committee to teach in the Friends Girls School in Ramallah, Palestine. I had met Khalil Totah, headmaster of the Friends Schools in Ramallah, at a Friends World Committee for Consultation conference, and in my senior year at college I applied for a position at the school.

In this record of my year as a teacher there, I have chosen to include not only experiences in the school and in Ramallah, but also my travels across the Atlantic Ocean and in the Middle East and Europe during that year. My journeys were an extension of my experience in Ramallah and provided a wider context for some of the political issues I faced daily there.

Commercial travel overseas in the late 1930s was limited to ocean liners and on-ground travel in Europe, and to buses and trains in the Middle East. These adventures — recorded in letters and journal entries — open a window on a pace of life that has all but disappeared today. Other tourists were scarce in these countries then, because of continuing wars in the Middle East and the threat of war in Europe.

It was my first extended period away from a rather sheltered Quaker environment. Country life and camping trips had fostered my love of adventure, and the turbulent year in Palestine fulfilled that need.

I grew up in Baltimore, the fifth child among seven siblings. My father was a businessman for a company that made hydraulic pumps and dredges. I suppose we were well off, but Quakers do not talk much about money. We lived simply and comfortably, winters in the city and summers at our farm in the hills of Maryland. The big, old house, lawns and orchards, the woods and swimming pond, the huge barn and outbuildings were an ideal place for children. There was no electricity; kerosene lamps made a gentle glow in the evenings as we read together or sang folk songs on the south porch.

The big adventure each year, a camping trip in the Appalachian Mountains, must have been an ordeal for my parents and the relatives who came along. There was no lightweight camping equipment in the 1930s, no sleeping bags, portable stoves, coolers, no zippers, no plastics. There were no state parks or tidy campgrounds; we always found a nice place in the woods, cleared away the weeds, and pitched camp.

"Now watch out for snakes," Dad would say. "There are copperheads around here." He liked to scare us a little. I loved the wilderness, the hiking, the singing, Aunt Lou with her box of cookies, Uncle Doctor with his snake-bite kit. I never liked fishing, tramping barelegged through the stinging nettles (little girls did not wear long pants), sitting quietly waiting for a fish to bite.

Several generations of my family had attended the Quaker boarding school, Westtown, near Philadelphia. It was almost a second home. The three years I spent at Westtown were a growing up and turning point in my life. I found I was not just a younger sister, I was a person with talents. The friends I made there have been a rich part of my life. At Goucher College in Baltimore I was a day student majoring in biology. Summers I spent with Westtown friends at a work camp on the coast of Maine.

After all these experiences, I was ready for the challenges of the year in Palestine. I was not very politically sophisticated, however, and I soon learned that although my Arab friends in Ramallah did not welcome the Jewish immigrants taking over their homeland, the war that we all endured there in 1939 was not Arabs against the Jews. It was Arabs against the British who, in 1938, still held a mandate of control over the entire country of Palestine. The rather naïve British soldiers stationed in Ramallah looked upon the natives as wayward children, deserving no respect for their life-style or their culture. Thus the British had set a pattern of behavior later adopted by the modern militant Israelis who now control much of the former Arab territory, destroying the ancient Arab homeland and rich culture.

My experience of Palestine was happily enhanced by the friendship of my companion and roommate, Gertrude McCoy of Ohio. Gertrude, also having her first year in Ramallah, was a recent graduate of Wilmington College. She had had a year of teaching music and had brought with her the warmth and grace of her supportive family. We met shipboard on the *Rex* going over and lived and traveled together for the entire year. Thanks for her never-failing good humor and her, "Yes, let's go."

I have not returned to Palestine since 1939, when Ramallah was a village where most of the people wore native dress, where there were more camels than cars on the roads and there were olive orchards on the hillsides, and where women sang at their work. I have lived in the Midwest as a teacher, wife, and mother in the community of Earlham College in Richmond, Indiana.

I had no camera in Palestine. Sometimes I sketched, but reading over my journals and letters soon after my return to the

United States, I made drawings to remind me of the people and activities of that eventful year. I was glad to be home, and yet I was homesick, missing my friends, the warmth, and even the grief of the Arab people I knew.

There are times when one's life seems to move in the fast lane. The experience of Palestine was, for me, an end to the easy days of fun, friends, and family protection. I was twenty-two, and the excellent education my parents had given me made it easy to relate to the wider world and to appreciate a staunch and beautiful people who, in the setting of Palestine's bare hills, were, and still are, struggling to save their precious culture, their homes, and their lives.

I think often of my former Arab students: bright, fun-loving, hopeful — their children and grandchildren, brought up in fear, losing their ancestral homes, their orchards, and perhaps even confined to the crowded refugee camps somewhere on the West Bank.

I dedicate to them, my former students and their families, these recollections of a way of life that is past. May they find the strength, forgiveness, and peace to incorporate the beauty of their traditions, their language, and their wisdom into the changing world that awaits us all.

Nancy Parker McDowell
November 2001

NOTES FROM RAMALLAH, 1939

Nancy Parker and Gertrude McCoy aboard the Rex

September–December, 1938

September 10 –17, 1938
On Board the *Rex*
Dear Family,

Thanks for the wonderful send-off party from Pier 92. I felt quite blue waving as we sailed out of New York harbor past the Statue of Liberty, and in half an hour we were out of sight of land. A whole year! When I found my cabin filled with flowers, letters, and gifts from so many people I was considerably cheered. My roommate, Gertrude McCoy, also going to teach at F.G.S. had flowers, too. Imagine our crowded cabin with four other women and all that stuff. The *Rex* is very Italian: food, crew, staff, and most of the passengers. There are six of us Americans going to Ramallah: besides Gertrude and me, two older women who are going back to teach and two young men going to teach at the Friends Boys School.

Life on board is quite fun. We third-class passengers are given deck space in the bow among the anchors and winches. We also have a small lounge and a dining room. Gertrude and I are sometimes invited up to second class for dancing in the evenings with second-class passengers, "Bella Senoritas" they call us. I guess they are short of women, but we like the third-class passengers

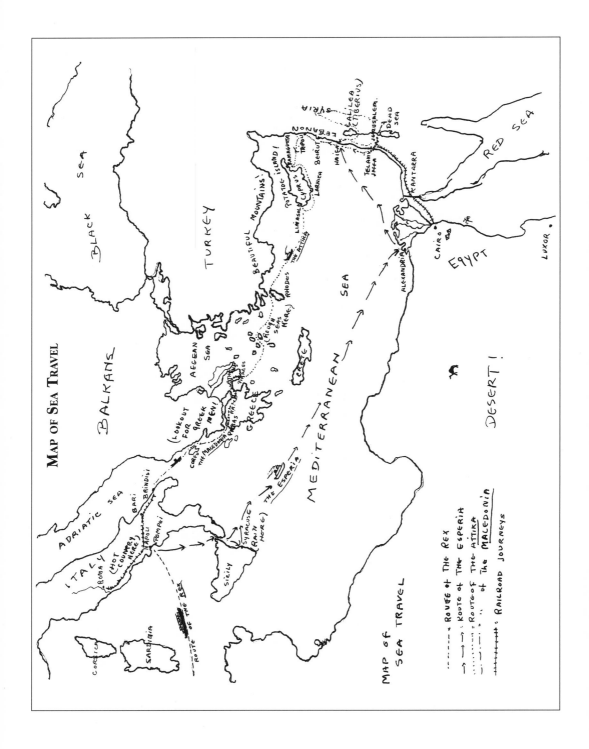

better. Yesterday, from the room next to ours, we heard singing, real Italian singing. It was Benito and Frankie, bass and tenor. They invited us in and gave us a concert as we sat on their bunks.

Third day: After we crossed the gulf stream (flying fish everywhere), the weather became stormy; decks and floors were sanded to keep us from slipping and ropes to hold as we staggered along the passages. Poor Frankie is terribly seasick. All his pep wilted away and he can only moan "How soon do we get to Napoli?" Benito and I sat by his bed and sang to him.

The fourth day at sea: We have passed the Azores, mountainous in the distance, then on through the open seas, another day 'til we come to the Mediterranean.

Fifth Day: "Portugal! Portugal!" Someone is shouting in the dining room. As we came nearer to land the water changed from blue to green. Great red cliffs loomed along the coast. We stopped off shore at Gibraltar to let on some passengers who came out in a small boat. But where is the famous Rock? After we cleared the harbor we looked back at the town twinkling in the darkness, and there was the rock of Gibraltar, huge and black against the starry sky. High up on the top was a red light like a warning. Is it saying, "Don't go into the Mediterranean?" It is the first time I have felt uneasy about going to the Middle East.

Sixth Day: Big dance on board this evening, and I danced with the Sheik of Morocco, he in his white and silver outfit and red fez. I, of course, gorgeous in my little cotton dress.

Seventh Day, Naples: The pier lined with soldiers in Robin Hood-type hats, Mussolini's merry men, we call them. We have a whole day to spend here, explore the steep narrow back streets with house doors opening onto the walkways, so everybody's living room includes the street where the women sit to do domestic chores. Through the open doors I could see many beds, people on balconies gossiping with those in the street. What a cozy community.

We went to Pompeii, passed the still smoking Vesuvius, and back in time to board the *Esperia*, bound for Alexandria and Haifa, where we will disembark after three more days at sea.

September 20, 1938

Dear family,

The *Esperia* is a much smaller boat than the *Rex*. We are six people to a cabin, rather hot and crowded with only one porthole. There is no lounge for third class passengers. All our deck space is filled up with cargo and refugees, who also fill up the baggage room. It smells pretty bad and makes us seasick. We spend most of our time in second class. But in third class are many interesting people. One young man told me he is a Jew from Vienna, who has escaped from Austria over the mountains with no money, no passport. There's something awful going on in Germany, so many people want to leave. Some Jews in Switzerland had helped him secure a passport. On the *Esperia* he was traveling deck passage and eating just the bit of food he had brought with him. He was going to Jerusalem, hoping to find a job and then study there at the Hebrew University. But he also had to send money to his people back home. The prospect of his future seemed hopeless.

Since it was too hot in our cabin last night, Gertrude and I slept up on first-class deck and nearly froze. About dawn I felt someone shaking me, shouting "Agua! Agua." The sailors were scrubbing the decks, rivers of water coming at us from all sides. We're approaching Haifa now. I'll have to finish this ashore.

The customs house

September 25, 1938

At Haifa the passport officials told us to go right back to America; nobody can enter Ramallah at this time. But once ashore, we were met by a man from the Friends School, Ussef Mozzowi, who helped us through customs without complications. One of us was chosen at random to be examined personally; a woman punched me all over to see if I carried firearms. We had to leave our Jewish friends, who must travel on Jewish buses and Jewish roads, while we went by Arab transport. We were asked to take off our hats (only Jewish women wear hats) and put on Arab headdress. It is safer to be Arab here, even though the British are on the side of the Jews. Ussef Mazzowi brought us chains of fresh jasmine as welcome gifts. He also brought us real American sandwiches.

We rode to Ramallah in a rather rickety bus, often passing towns that the British had bombed because of insurrections. In one village a hundred and seventy houses had been bombed. All that was left were the messy piles of stone. Because some Arabs in that village had killed a British commander, the British gave them twenty hours notice and then bombed the village. British encampments are all along the road and soldiers ride around with machine guns.

All this military business doesn't spoil the charm of Palestine. It is a country of bare rocky hills with goats grazing on the dry tufts of grass. Camel trains and laden donkeys are more common than cars. Most of the people dress just as they did in biblical times, living in the same houses and in the same way. Bedouin tents are sprinkled along the plains, and Bedouin women with tattooed faces grovel about for scraps of food like gypsies.

The trip from Haifa to Ramallah took about three hours, counting the frequent breakdowns of the bus and the running out of "benzene." Then we had to stop several times while all the men climbed out and were searched for firearms by British soldiers. They don't search women any more. The day before we arrived in Palestine, Arabs threw a big strike over the way British soldiers were treating Palestinian women. We were lucky to arrive when we did; the previous day buses weren't running because of the strike, and the day after, they had another big strike in memory of a rebel leader who had been killed. In the past week, Ramallah has become a rebel town, having thrown over British rule. All post office and telephone communications are cut off from the town. The bus, of course, did not go into Ramallah. From Bireh, we had to walk the last mile and a half. Our trunks were brought in by  camel the next day. British soldiers picket the outskirts and the radio station. No one goes out of the house at night and there is official curfew on all the main roads of Palestine. The first night in Ramallah I went to bed hearing machine guns firing just a few blocks away.

We have two weeks before school starts, but we can't travel around and visit the historic sights. From Ramallah we can see the Mount of Olives and Jerusalem and the mountains of Moab. Yesterday we went into Jerusalem with Dr. Totah to register with the American Consul. Although it is unsafe to go inside the walls of the old city (the new city is built around it), we had to go in for one errand. While we were there a policeman stopped us and asked if we were Jews. The new Jews in this country are not like American Jews, but light, like myself. He was going to arrest us for being in that part of the city. We should have worn Arab dress. Sometimes people spit at us, but they haven't hit yet.

We get our mail from Jerusalem every day, but there are no newspapers available, just when we want them most. We talk and think of nothing but the situation in Europe. By the time you get this letter you will know whether there is to be war. We listen to news from London and Berlin. None of them agree about what is going on.

Next week sometime, Ramallah is expecting six hundred British soldiers to be stationed in the town, taking over two old hotels. They say it is to keep down the rebels, but really we think it is because Mussolini wants to snatch Egypt and these soldiers are ready to dash down there and keep the Suez from falling into Italy's hands.

Life in Ramallah is interesting, even when there is no fighting going on. The town has an Oriental atmosphere. Women in beautifully embroidered dresses and head shawls walk around with huge jugs or baskets on their heads. The women who work in our kitchen are typical. They are always barefoot, walking on the cold stone floors. When we walk around the town we are often scolded because we don't wear headdress and long sleeves as proper women do. I guess we will have to conform. Women never speak to a man on the street.

There are two classes of people in Ramallah; the educated, business class, who speak English and send their children to the Friends Schools and live in large, stone houses with bathrooms and brightly upholstered furniture. Then there are the "falaheen," who live in old, old stone houses and wrest a living from

the unyielding land. These houses are built around stone-paved courtyards, where neighbor women work together. Each home has one living room, kept very clean, and below it is a store room, where are kept provisions and the family donkey. There are large clay bins and jugs for oil and water. The women carry water from the town wells.

The streets of Ramallah are lined with shops, and clattering with donkeys, or flocks of goats and jolly people. On our way to buy figs one day, G. and I heard a rhythmical beating as of some primitive, tuneless instrument. In a small shop we found the town cotton fluffer, half buried in a pile of white softness, beating cotton across his one stringed instrument. The air was sneezy with floating down. Every year people bring their soggy pillows to be fluffed. To the rhythm of his instrument we, of course, made up a song and dance. From a weaver we bought some hand loomed linen to embroider in the traditional Ramallah cross stitch patterns.

The peasants walk miles to their strips of stony land in the valleys. In the rainy season they take the donkey to plow and plant. Each family has two or three olive trees. Ripe olives are deep purple among the dull green leaves, a soft color to enrich the red-brown hills. The men beat the trees and the women pick up the olives and carry them home in bags or baskets, on their heads. If there is a large crop, they place some on the donkey, and even the man must walk.

Now, about politics. The war in Palestine is most complicated; but this is how I understand it, so far:

After the world war, in 1918, when Britain acquired Palestine from the Turks, she promised, in the Balfour Declaration, to give it to the Jews as a national homeland. At the same time she promised independence to the Arabs, who have occupied Palestine for the past five thousand years. Now both are demanding full rights to govern themselves, and the British have placed the country under military control. In the past few years some of the Arabs, under leadership of the Mufti (a Moslem chief), have taken to violent rebellion against British authority. These are "The Rebels," or Arab terrorists, who have just taken over Ramallah.

I have taken to doing cross-stitch work like other Ramallah women. I never thought I would come to it, but it keeps you from thinking too much.

Love, Nance

> *Now that commercial air travel has reduced the distance between Jerusalem and New York City from ten days to ten hours and e-mail brings instant communication, it is poignant to remember how remote we felt out there in the Near East. This distance added much to the excitement of being, and the urge to write about it. My family enthusiastically received these letters, copied and passed them around. The letters are now yellow and brittle with age — sixty-two years. It is a different world, there and here, then and now.*

Observations from my journal
October 8, 1938

Gertrude and I don't know whether we should tell our parents about the battle last Saturday. Early in the morning we found the town was full of rebel soldiers who had gathered during the night. They looked like ordinary Arabs, but they carried guns, which they had stolen from the British police. It is unlawful for an Arab to carry arms. Usually when caught they are hanged. That afternoon, as G. and I were going over to the classroom building, we saw four men inside the school gate, crouching behind the wall. They all had guns. Soon they jumped over the wall and ran up the hill opposite our school, where great clouds of smoke poured forth. We heard shooting at the top of the hill. British soldiers had come to attack all the rebels in town. We ran up on the roof to see better. It was true guerilla warfare, rebels running from all sides in disorganized groups. The odds are terrible, because the British use machine guns.

As we watched the sight from the roof, we heard the bark of a machine gun rather close, and a bullet whizzed by. Almost before we knew it we were inside the building. Rebels began to run through our yard, and the school janitor, Owie, came in to take us to the main building. We made a dash between the running rebels and were safe inside, just as the shooting began again. After a while the noise of machine guns became so steady we didn't even dare to peek out of the windows. We crouched on the floor, I don't know how long, but, finally, the fight moved to another part of town. The machine gun truck drove away with a bunch of healthy-looking British soldiers sitting up as boldly as if there weren't a hundred rebels trying to shoot them down. Only one man was killed in our vicinity. We could see the rest of the fight from our balcony, until six British planes flew over and dropped some bombs, looking like huge eggs falling from the belly of the plane.

About eighty Arabs were killed. Of the British, only one, our friend, Sargent Birch, was killed. He had taken refuge in the house of our laundress, where the Arabs shot him down and burned the house. The poor widow who owned it had worked years and just finished building her home. All the rest of the day, planes flew low over the town. The rebels had taken cover, some in the houses of friends, others escaping to the valleys. The British also bombed some innocent people who were only running home from their vineyards. Two women and three men were killed.

On Sunday morning we couldn't go to church, because they were still popping off at a few people in the center of town. In the afternoon things were pretty quiet and we went to see the bullet holes in the neighbors' houses. Our building had only one pockmark that we could find. The roads had been blocked off with rocks so that British armored cars couldn't get by. Burned houses were still smoldering, rebel soldiers skulking about, but the British had departed. We couldn't get radio news, and telephone wires had been cut. Palestine's radio station is situated at Ramallah, and controlled by the British. Broadcasts are all telephoned from Jerusalem. It's just as well; if news of the battle gets all over Palestine, nobody will send their children to the opening of the Friends Schools next week.

Report written to Homewood Meeting, Baltimore.
October 9, 1938

I am sitting on a balcony of the Friends Girls School, looking out across brown hills that roll on and on until they become a hazy mist in the Mediterranean Sea. To the south, only ten miles away, lies Jerusalem, hidden by hills where the Friends Boys School stands. Ramallah is a town of yellow houses, pink roofs. Every available foot of land is planted with vineyards and low, yellow stone walls mark the boundaries of each family's property. In the older part of Ramallah are crooked, narrow streets, paved with stones. The buildings are so ancient that their stone thresholds are worn in deep hollows. We often meet donkeys, heavily laden, or flocks of sheep and goats coming in from the meager grazing that these bleak hills offer. This is the dry season, everything parched and dusty. The women of Ramallah are picturesque in their long gowns, cross stitched with bright red, and silken shawls over their heads. They carry on their heads baskets of grapes, or jugs of water balanced with perfect poise.

School has been in session here only two days. This year we have a smaller enrollment than usual, because Ramallah has recently been the center of political troubles. The students are all Arab children from Christian and Moslem families. I am already very fond of them. As people of the East they have beautiful manners and, in the classroom, more enthusiasm than American youngsters. The younger children are taught in Arabic, but from kindergarten up all are drilled in English. After the seventh grade, they do all of their studies in English. We American teachers must keep reminding ourselves they are working in a foreign language.

There are four American teachers in the school: Annice Carter, of Indiana Yearly Meeting, and Garnet Guild of Oregon have taught here for several years; Gertrude McCoy of Ohio and I are new teachers. I am the youngest teacher and am sometimes mistaken for a student, but students wear uniforms. Victoria Hannush, director of the Girls School, is a good executive with gentle dignity and a charming sense of humor, a perfect headmistress.

In the Boys School are two new American teachers, Elmore Leppert and Roger Hawley, both from the West. We Americans all came over on the boat together and were well acquainted before arriving in Palestine. Mildred White, from Indiana, now teaches in the Boys School and Khalil Totah is the principal of both schools.

In our school the girls rise at six in the morning and do all the housework before their morning classes. Otherwise the school is very much like American schools. When classes are over at three thirty, the teachers can relax with their tea before going out to supervise games and athletics. My own schedule includes teaching ancient history, Medieval history, geography of Europe, geography of the world, biology, general science, sixth-grade English, and hygiene. It is not such a heavy schedule as it seems, for it only amounts to twenty-one hours in the classroom a week. We also supervise athletics, housework and take personal charge of a group of fifteen "daughters." And I have a Sunday School class, which I enjoy very much. I find my hardest job is to be a model of neatness and promptness. Last year in college I thought I could not possibly be busier, or have so many responsibilities; but compared with teaching, college is a life of leisure. I am also learning a great deal.

Political conditions in this country are, of course, our chief interest outside of school. Living in the midst of conflict and danger gives one a new perspective. We are not fearful, but we are alert. Last evening at dinnertime I was startled by the sound of the children's chairs scraping on the stone floor as they took their places. It sounded just like the machine guns we frequently hear.

Since Ramallah has become a rebel town (against the British government), our post office and all our telephones have been removed. Fortunately the buses to Jerusalem have been reinstated and run fairly regularly, about once a day. On Arab buses going to and from the main cities British officers search men for arms. It is a capital offense for Arabs to carry weapons of any kind. Every day we hear of people being shot in Palestine cities and land mines exploding under buses on main roads. There are curfews on all the roads of Palestine. Even where there are no official curfews, no one ventures out after dark. From our school we often hear the British machine guns that guard the radio station.

Last Saturday (October 1) Arab rebels from all over the country gathered in Ramallah and were attacked by the British. We were glad that our students had not yet arrived and that the stone walls of our school are two feet thick. To have rebels charging across your yard is exciting for a while, but the sound of machine guns close by becomes annoying. Although neither British nor Arabs have any objection to the American Friends Mission School, they are not always careful where they aim their guns. We were torn between curiosity to watch the battle from our windows and fear of being hit by a stray bullet. We would peep cautiously from our windows and then duck down behind the wall when the noise came too close. We have only found one place where the building was struck. After a few hours some British planes flew over the village and dropped bombs on the thickest of the battle. The Arabs were then forced to disperse. We heard later that about eighty lives were lost. The only arms the Arabs have are rifles that have been stolen from the British. It seems futile for them to try to fight against the highly organized British army with its planes and machine guns. The temperament of both Jews and Arabs is such that they cannot settle their issue peaceably. It seems a hopeless deadlock, but we still hope for peace. We are all anxious to hear the outcome of the conference that is now being held in Egypt and concerns the welfare of all British mandates. The Ramallah Monthly Meeting of Friends has sent a cable of appreciation to Neville Chamberlain and asked that he might next direct his attention to the peaceful solution of Palestine's problem. Realizing that this is only a feeble gesture, we still feel that it is in keeping with the practice of the Society of Friends.

Gertrude

October 12, 1938

Dear Mother,

Students are arriving this morning, while I sit and make lesson plans. I am teaching eight subjects, two history, two science, English, health, two geography. I also teach a Sunday school class, have to give a chapel speech once a week and supervise fifteen girls (cleanliness, laundry, keep account of their money and health). I supervise the cleaning of several class rooms (the students do the work) and one day a week am on duty all day to supervise the activities of all the girls from dawn 'til bed time. I also teach baseball. Imagine me — baseball!

Gertrude and I room together, which is very nice, because the Arab teachers get on our nerves sometimes, probably because of our ignorance of the language, and they are very excitable. No wonder, when their country is being torn apart. We are having an awful time with fleas. We seem to have picked them up somewhere, off the streets I guess, because this building is clean enough. I am covered with bites, but I never can catch the fleas. In fact, I haven't seen one yet.

The food is quite good and the climate makes us hungry all the time, even though we get no exercise. We have lots of rice, cooked with pine nuts and other things. We have many vegetables from the squash family, and egg plant, cooked with meat and rice, "batinjan-mashill" they call it. The bread is wonderful, flat loaves baked in out-door stone ovens. The cheeses are strong and sour, often made with sheep milk, but I have learned to like them especially with marmalade. They use lots of olive oil, poured over things and to dunk the bread. There is no butter. The cows give skim milk, I think. The teachers only eat with the students at noon meal, except the teacher on duty, who is with them all day.

Most of the girls I teach will be high-school age. Tomorrow is my first day of teaching. It is hard to prepare for a class when I don't yet know what teaching is like. Wish I had taken some Ed. courses in college. The students come from well-to-do homes; many of them arrive in automobiles, which you don't see often around here. Most people get about on donkeys or camels. There are some ten porters hanging around fighting over who shall carry the bags. They only get half a piaster a bag, but that is how they make a living. They are quite dirty. Arabs fight over the least little thing, or maybe that is just their way of relating; their language sounds like fighting. Many of our students are Moslem girls and arrive with their faces covered by a black veil. In school they do not need to veil.

Yesterday I smelled a most heavenly smell from the back porch. There was our cook, squatting by a small charcoal stove, roasting coffee beans. Our cooks are Ramallah women who wear long dress, cross stitched in black and red, bright girdle around the middle, orange shawl over the head and bare feet. I don't know how they keep warm on the stone floors. Even my bedroom has a stone floor. Everything is stone, houses, streets, walls around vineyards. It's one commodity that is plentiful in this country.

Love,
Nance

October 14, 1938

Dear Mother,

Thy letters have been welcome spots in my weeks. American mail comes once a week, and so far I have not been disappointed. We were worried about the hurricane, mentioned very briefly in the news. It is the only news of America we have had. The radio is full of Europe, and we can't read the Arabic papers, which are only printed occasionally because of Arab strikes. Since the Jews are always having feasts and holidays, we do not get much news from them.

I have been teaching a week and a half now and today is my heaviest day, my day "on duty." I am responsible for all the girls' activities. I rise at 5:30, ring the wake up bell at six, and then go up and shake the girls awake. They sleep in two big dormitories, the big girls in one room and the younger girls in the other, with an Arab teacher. Arab girls are very modest and always dress under the covers. They emerge in slip and put on their school uniform. When I ring my little bell at 6:20, they kneel down and say their prayers. Then they roll back their bedcovers neatly and go downstairs to help get breakfast. My job was to fish the bees out of the honey and cut up the pieces of sour white cheese in strips. Every morning a woman comes from the vineyards with a basket of grapes on her head. I wish I had a picture of her. For breakfast we had bread and cheese, tea and grapes.

Later: Now I am sitting at the end of a long table supervising evening study hour. The girls study so ferociously they whisper to themselves and do not realize it; a hum of whispering can be heard all over the room. But when they whisper to each other I can notice the difference, because they keep looking at me. Usually they are very orderly. At meal times they line up outside the dining room without a word. When I give the signal they march in and stand quietly at their places. I had to learn the

Arabic prayer so that I could start the grace. At noon all the teachers eat with the girls, each of us sitting at the head of a table. We get much better food when we eat by ourselves at breakfast and tea. The girls have beautiful manners. When I enter the classroom they stand and say, "Good morning, Miss Parker." Only they say Miss Barker. They can't pronounce "P." At the end of class they stand and say, "Thank you, Miss Barker." They often bring me flowers and, because I teach science, loathsome lizards and beetles.

After dinner today I supervised mending. The students taught me Arabic songs as they sewed. At supper there was some kind of bean dish, which they all hated, preferring the bread and jam. I was supposed to see that they ate a little of the beans. Well, say the other teachers, it is as good as they get at home.

On Saturdays we have to see that they all have baths. Arabs don't like to use bathtubs; it is unsanitary. They have a little place like a shower, only with no running water. The hired man makes a fire in a little stove, which heats a boiler full of water. Then the student helper and teacher on duty carry buckets of water around and fill the pitchers in each "shower" compartment. The girls go in one at a time, pull the curtain tight, sit on a little stool and, with a tin cup, proceed to pour water over themselves. We teachers have a tub bath once a week and every night at bedtime we fill our hot water bottles at the kitchen stove. In the morning we wash in the lukewarm water from the h.w. bottles.

Every teacher has a group of girls to inspect each morning. We examine the day students especially carefully for lice. I haven't found any yet, but maybe I don't know how to look. This morning one of the teachers found a bed bug in a girl's bed. She had brought her mattress from home. Every girl had to hang her mattress out on the balcony.

The East winds have come, bringing a spell of hot weather and sand flies, the itchiest bugs I have met, even after years of camping in Maine. We sleep under mosquito netting, but still they bite.

Our trials are easier to bear because Gertrude and I room together. She is the music teacher, has a pleasant alto voice, and we sing duets. Last Sunday in church-meeting we sang "In the Garden" for part of the service. Meeting is half in Arabic, half in English. When Gertrude plays the piano for the Arabic hymns, she has to read the music backwards, as Arabic reads. The language is beginning to make some sense to me.

Saturday: There is no place for me to go because the girls are cleaning everywhere. In our room a little girl is scrubbing the stone floor and the mattresses are hanging in the sun. There has been more trouble with bed bugs since some new girls came this week. They are sunning all the dormitory beds, spray everybody's suitcase and closet, and wash all the bedsprings with kerosene. Just now one of the teachers tried to go to Jerusalem, but after two kilometers the bus driver turned back because, by some mysterious means, he got word that there is shooting in Jerusalem and a British person was killed. There is no use discussing the political situation any more. It is always the same,

me — portrait by That Syrian Artist

more people killed, more towns bombed. The rebels came to the Boys School this morning and stole all their typewriters, which they need for sending messages. The Boys School sent a runner to warn us to hide ours. We have also hidden our money; we wrap it up in our undergarments. The rebel Arabs would never look through a lady's personal things. Today or tomorrow we are going to hike over to a hill where you can look down onto the Jordan and the Dead Sea.

Monday Morning: Yesterday after meeting, Mildred White invited Gertrude and me to dinner at the Boys School. After dinner she took Gertrude and Elmore and Roger and me to a Greek Orthodox baptism, at the home of some people she knew. We Americans were the honored guests. The house was seething with people and little children with sore eyes. A large tureen was placed on a stand of hammered copper and a very dirty priest appeared. The baby was cuddled and kissed by everyone and then the godfather held it while the priest made signs over it and read the Arabic service. They closed all the windows and waved incense around until the room was very stuffy. Then they undressed the baby, sprinkled oil on it and the priest sort of folded it up and dunked it in the water, completely under, three times. The poor baby squalled and everybody laughed and the priest kept right on

The three Greek priests

muttering. In the Greek Orthodox Church nobody pays any attention to the service, you just talk and laugh and scold your children all through it. They dressed the baby in lots of ruffles and sweaters and gave everybody a candle, then we all paraded around the baptismal font, chanting a song and waving our tapers. We were served rich pastry and liqueur, everybody drinking from the same goblet, and some thick black coffee.

That night Mrs. Totah gave a party for one of the staff of the Boys School who is leaving. Because of curfew she invited Gertrude and me to stay all night. We had a real American supper and a real American evening. We sang, told tall stories, talked politics, of course, and ate popcorn, a rare treat in this country.

Since the British soldiers are now staying in Ramallah, there has been a good bit of shooting in the valleys. One night at midnight, Gertrude and I went up to the high balcony where we could see the rebels flashing signals across the hills. They send up bright things like sky rockets, but they make a brighter light. We often hear the distant rumble of land mines and bombs going off, only we cannot tell any more what are bombs and what are not. Last night there was a terrific boom that brought us both out of bed. The next day we found that the top floor of one of our neighbor's houses had become so rickety from age it had just fallen down. Nobody was hurt; they had been expecting it for years.

Another noise that makes us shake in our beds is the howling of jackals that come in from the hills for garbage. It sounds like frightened children shrieking. We don't mind the guns nearly as much, in fact we sleep right through most of it. But we are pretty shot-conscious by this time. Every time a door slams or a desk shuts we think it is a shot. Last night a teacher was reading aloud to some of the girls when some shots went off fairly near the school. She did not hear them because she was reading, but when she looked up she found them all crouched on the floor. The first reaction on hearing a shot is to lie down below the window level.

Don't worry about us. Nobody wants to shoot us.

> *If my daughter wrote this to me today, I would insist that she come home immediately. However, in 1939 there was no way to come home immediately. I don't think I really appreciated the anxiety I must have inflicted on my parents in Baltimore.*

Journal Entry
October 20, 1938

Notes gleaned from tea-table talk about politics:

Before 1918 Palestine had been ruled by Turkey for three hundred years. After World War I, in the Treaty of Versailles, the British were given a mandate over Palestine. They (the British) made two treaties. One promised the Arabs freedom to rule their country. Two years later the British Balfour Declaration promised the Jews Palestine for a homeland. Now they can't decide which treaty to break. America (F.D.R.) has reaffirmed the Balfour Declaration, especially encouraging Jewish immigration to Palestine. Wealthy and influential American Jews are supporting the Zionist movement, putting pressure on England to keep the treaty with Jews.

Arabs are divided into two parties, the Mufti Party and the "Rebels." Both oppose the Jews and Britain, but I am not sure how they differ with each other. There is an enormous cultural clash between Arabs and the new Jews in Palestine (A small group of "Orthodox Jews" has lived here peaceably with Arabs these two thousand years.). The Eastern, or Arab, culture is conservative and deep and includes both Moslems and Eastern Orthodox

Christians. The new Jews who have come in since the war (World War I) have brought undesirable aspects of Western culture, (freedom of women and immodest dress, cinema, venereal disease, and fast living) to this country of long-established traditions. If the British break their treaty with the Arabs, the Arabs will kill the Jews; if they break treaty with the Jews, Jews will kill the Arabs. Both have a long-term claim to the country. They cannot live together because of their differences in worldview. Arabs don't want to become a modern progressive nation, whereas Jews have a marvelous talent for progress.

In my feeble Arabic, I had a political discussion with the donkey driver who brings water to fill our well:

Donkey Driver: "Harame, you are American, you don't like the Arabs."

Me: "Why do you say that? The Arabs are my friends."

D.D.: "But your President Roosevelt, he loves Jews. He wants to give Palestine to the Jews."

Me: "President Roosevelt doesn't know about the Arabs in Palestine." (I can't say "situation" in Arabic.)

D.D. "Your America. Why do you let the Jews run everything in your country?"

Me: *"Barafish"* (I don't know.) I had run out of language and ideas.

Ever since Roosevelt has been meddling in Palestine's affairs with his cables to the British government, advising them regarding Jewish immigration in Palestine, Americans in Palestine have not been held in such high favor among Arabs as they were. The American consul announces over the radio every night that all American citizens must register with him, a thing we attended to the first week we were here.

My friend Cedric writes from Basel University on the German border, "No one here speaks of pacifism. Everyone feels that war with Germany is inevitable."

October 24, 1938

Dear Rachel:

Thanks for thy letter and thanks again for the lovely dinner at thy home the night before I sailed. I'm afraid I will not be able to visit thy friend Mrs. Jacobs. The place where she lives is a Jewish colony about half a day's journey from Ramallah. I would love to visit her, but when I mentioned it at tea the Arab teachers protested furiously, telling me I had better not go near that place or I would be murdered. I keep forgetting I am supposed to be afraid of Jews, but if things ever calm down, I will go. I would like to see the Jewish side of things.

At present it would be impossible to attempt a journey to Tel Aviv. Only Arab buses run, and they wouldn't go near Jewish colonies. Even if I could get there I would be an object of suspicion in Ramallah. Anyway it isn't safe to travel anywhere on Jewish or Arab roads. I doubt if I could even get to Haifa or Jaffa to take a boat home if I had to. There's a rumor around today that all transportation in Palestine is to be discontinued entirely for about a week. Things are a mess here. Thee said the papers mentioned a battle in the "Ramallah mountains." The battle was right in our back yard and it was not Arabs against Jews, it was Arabs against British. The battle has been going on ever since, sometimes in the valleys and sometimes in our streets. But now, most of the fighting is at night.

There is a curfew in the town from 7 p.m. to 5 a.m. As soon as the rebel Arabs have had their tea they get out their little guns and proceed to pop them off at the British. Last Saturday about six hundred British soldiers moved into town, taking over the two old hotels and the government school. They cut down all the trees near their barracks and tore down the walls so that nobody could sneak up on them unseen. All day long the sentries pace the roof of the hotel on Main Street, bayonet in hand. They don't even put their guns on their shoulders, but hold them ready to shoot. Their machine-gun trucks drive around all cocked, to scare people into obedience. But the Ramallah people go about their business with their donkeys and camel trains just as usual. Then at night they put sandbags on their windows to keep out the bullets. My desk is right by the window. I study there until the shooting begins, and then I shift to the floor. Pretty chilly there.

Gertrude and I are getting quite good at distinguishing between the sound of rebel rifles and the British. "Sounds as if the British are getting ahead tonight," we say. But mostly we sleep through the racket. If it gets too close, we go upstairs to the girls' dormitory and calm their fears.

The father of one of our girls was killed last week. We heard about it through some way that Khalil Totah has of getting news from the rebels. We can't tell the girl yet because there is no way she could get home and we don't want it to spread all over the school. He was a well-known man among Arabs. Today was the first day we could get mail from Jerusalem for a week. The poor girl is wondering why she didn't get her weekly letter from him.

I am eagerly awaiting the announcement of the arrival of my first niece/nephew. I am sending thee this blue bead, which thee must hang around the infant's neck to keep away the evil eye. I have seen several small children wearing the blue bead. It especially protects them from blue-eyed people, whose glance is fraught with evil. Poor blond Gertrude has beautiful blue eyes.

Love, Nance

Journal Entry
November 1938

Local Gossip: Since the Yorkshire regiment has moved into Ramallah, staying in two hotels, we have a new Mayor, British. I suppose they know Ramallah is the rebel center and Mr. Gordan, the mayor, is determined to find their leader, Abu Hassam. The rebels are out to get the mayor, but don't want to kill him in Ramallah, which would bring down a heavy retribution on our town. The British usually bomb towns where a British is killed. The British frequently detain Arab citizens, keeping them in a concentration camp for several days, hoping they may find the leader. Permits are required of all Arabs in hopes of finding who are rebels and who are not, but the rebels won't let anybody get permits.

Late in the winter we could not go to the valleys for flowers, because the rebels were getting worse. They posted a list of names of Ramallah people who had not contributed enough money to the rebel cause and threatened that if these men should come out of their houses they would be killed. One night some British soldiers found a group of men in a Ramallah coffee house after curfew. These men were rebel leaders and had been planning an attack on the British. They concealed their rifles in the long, loose garments of the old blind man who was keeper of the coffee house. Possession of armaments is a capital offense. Puzzled at finding a group of Arabs together at such an hour, the British took them off to the concentration camp, except for the harmless old blind fellow, who had the rifles concealed under his garments. The next day Ramallah was in a secret uproar. "They have taken Abu Hassam, our Arab leader. Now he will be hung." Abu Hassam was seen heavily guarded, carrying stones in the concentration camp.

Men could not go out of their houses without being picked up by soldiers. The prisoners were allowed to sleep inside the government boys' school, but they had no covers those cold nights. In the daytime we could see a long line of them working for the British, tearing down the stone walls their ancestors had built between fields. The British were trying to build a high, modern wall around their barracks, which means they must intend to stay in Ramallah permanently. The soldiers never found out they had in their custody the chief rebel leaders and Abu Hassam; they let them go.

Ramallah men can't go to work in their orchards and fields and the women can't pick the olives alone because it is difficult to beat and shake the trees. During these hard days we had a few days' truce for the men to pick the olives, but they could not get much done before the six o'clock curfew.

One day we were wakened by shouting and tumult, "The British are going to search Ramallah." The whole town was in a panic. People hid their valuables on their persons. Our day students arrived carrying the family wealth and jewels because the American school is supposed to be a safe place. Gertrude and I stood in our room undecided whether to carry our money and passports around with us or not. Decided not. The people were all herded out of their houses into the streets. We went up to see the fun before school started and great was the weeping and wailing. The panic of the people was unnecessary because the soldiers did little damage, no ripping open of bags of wheat and the winters supply of oil this time. I asked a soldier why they were searching. He said, "I don't know, Miss, it's orders."

The community nurse, who is a brave soul and knows the soldiers, noticed they marked each house "S" after they had searched it. So the nurse went around with a piece of chalk and marked all the houses "S."

Since the British troops now occupy the two hotels in Ramallah, they have surrounded the buildings with barbwire fencing, cut down trees, and demolished walls that might hide any rebels. Anyone breaking the evening curfew is shot without question. The British general advises us to put sandbags in our windows to keep out stray bullets. When we ride to Jerusalem (ten miles) on the bus, we have to stop while British soldiers search all the male passengers for arms; sometimes they take their money. When our students came to school, their fathers brought the tuition money in their shoes.

In the village of Nablus there was a bank robbery last week. So the British herded all the inhabitants out to a field, where they had to stand in the hot sun all day while soldiers searched their houses. They rip up the furniture, dump out the food supplies and take all the money and valuable things they can find. One of our students from Nablus was unable to come back to school, because her father's jewelry shop was wiped out.

The rebels force the rich Arabs to give money for their cause, and two of the fathers of our students were shot because they refused. Last week the rebels took the old part of Jerusalem, the part within the walls. They found a secret entrance and smuggled arms in...then they walked through the Jaffa gate, allowing the soldiers to search them as usual. Once inside they grabbed their guns and closed the gates. They killed two British Egyptian spies and hung their heads over Damascus gate with a sign, "This for Traitors." There was curfew in the Old City day and night, and many of the poor people starved, unable to go out of their houses for food or even to bury the dead.

The British are now issuing a decree, which makes transportation practically impossible. Nobody can go to Jerusalem without a special permit and the rebels have threatened to shoot anybody who gets a permit. Buses are on strike. We are now doing without butter and fresh milk, and Ramallah is short of flour.

Since we hear that Roosevelt is favoring the Jewish cause, Americans are not so popular in Arab Palestine. We eight American teachers in the Friends Boys and Girls Schools are now prisoners in Ramallah until things ease up. We hope they will before Christmas so that we can go to Cairo. It is certainly an experience, living in a real war, having curfew, and getting used to the sound of guns at night.

> *I have since wondered why I wasn't more fearful. Perhaps because it wasn't my war. And youth does not really believe in danger. I had a strong sense of family security. I knew I would live to be an old woman.*

Sunday, December 3, 1938

Dear Mother:

This is December the third and I never felt less like Christmas, except that last week we did have fun wrapping our packages for home. Gertrude and I have been talking about the packages for weeks. We could only send a certain weight of stuff and only certain things that were not dutiable. I would like to get you some Ramallah cross-stitch work and some Jerusalem pottery, but those are things you cannot send. I am even thinking of getting a prayer rug for Johnny and Libby. Wouldn't that be a nice wedding present for them? Here the Moslem people actually use them. I was in a Moslem home one day and said "what a beautiful hanging." They said, "Oh, that is father's prayer rug." He prays five times a day, taking down his prayer rug and turning toward Mecca in the South. Some of our more strict Moslem students do too.

We have had a bad time because so many of the students fasted for a month before the feast of Ramadan. They can only eat at night, and then only a little. They have to get up at 3 a.m. to eat their sandwich, which they keep by their beds. Some of them got very weak and did poorly in their studies. But the month was over the day before Thanksgiving. You need not fear that I will join the Moslems! I am always hungry, and I am getting right roly-poly.

Letters! Letters! I read them over and over and then read them to Gertrude. She also reads me her letters from home, so we get double mail. This week I was the luckiest person in Ramallah, eight letters! One from Do, Ebie, Eric, Beck, Albert, Uncle Bert, Marian, and best of all one from thee, which I saved till last. I read them all but thine in my only free period on Friday. Then I still had something to look forward to after I taught my next two classes.

The latest *National Geographic* (December) has an article on Palestine. The pictures are just what we see every day. On page 706 the description of Tel Aviv tells what the Jews have brought to Palestine. They have too much money for the poor bewildered Arabs and have overpowered them before the Arabs realized what was happening. It says that Palestine is the dream country of the Jews for two thousand years. But the Jews only lived there a few centuries before they were scattered. And I should think the Arabs have a right to their own land, which they have cultivated and occupied since human beings came into that region.

It makes me sad that the Friends of Baltimore Meeting have signed that petition for the Jews to be given Palestine, when they don't know the situation. This does not mean I hate the Jews, as these Arabs do or that I do not realize that they have to have some place to go when they are being persecuted all over the world. But Palestine is too small for them, and people seem to forget about the Arabs who have always lived here and have just had their country given away to a foreign people by a foreign power.

The land is so barren that you have to eke out your existence. The native Arabs are slow and inefficient, compared with Jewish progressive ideas, but their traditions have been established by hundreds of generations. I am not so sure that the industrial progression, which the Jews represent, is the most worthwhile thing in life.

We still do not know whether we will have a Christmas vacation. We took no notice of Thanksgiving. If cars cannot run, and they haven't for the past month, the girls cannot go home. So we will just keep on with school until they can go home.

And I am on duty on Christmas Day! "Harame," the Arabs say when they mean "too bad." Just today a rumor has been spreading "Cars will start running again next Wednesday." But we have seen the rumor starting up so often that we are cynical.

Whatever happens, you may think of me on Christmas Day here at School. Gertrude and I are going to fill each other's socks. If all goes well we will start for Cairo right after Christmas, by train or by sea, we don't know which. If all doesn't go well we will go right on teaching the day after Christmas.

We are now having the biggest oranges I have ever seen. They are honestly as big as grapefruits at home. They have thick rough skins and are still sour and green. They come from Jaffa. We have also tiny little bananas from Jericho and tiny little bitter grapefruit from Gaza. The grapefruit are smaller than the oranges. Someone gave us a "ruttle" of dried figs last week; most of them are wormy but we ate the good part. Dried figs are not as pretty as those you get all wrapped up in cellophane. They are almost black and look awfully dirty sometimes. But we gobble them down. We have fresh dates too, they are delicious until they get too ripe. Then they get a bit alcoholic. We had today "Sfeha," a sort of flat bread-roll with meat on top. You eat it with leban, which we have nearly every meal. And every meal we have the sour, white cheese, which I love to eat with jam. All of our milk is boiled. I have not tasted ice cream for nigh unto three months now and haven't seen a movie.

The captain of the British battalion, stationed at the Ramallah Hotel has invited us to come up and see their American movies on Wednesday nights. We said, "We cannot on account of curfew." But he said if we could come he would send a special escort of armed soldiers to take us and bring us home. We don't think much of the low-class of British soldiers who wink at us on the streets of Ramallah. But the movies are exclusively for captains and lieutenants, so we think that would be fun.

There has been shooting lately, but it hasn't seemed near. Yesterday one of the Arab teachers and I were in charge of the Literary Program. We have been rehearsing the girls all week, and we had them sing two English songs, an Arabic song, give a folk dance, and then a little play that I happened to bring along. Afterwards I went with Teacher to visit a Moslem school, where they teach washing and ironing and gardening and cooking and sewing. The girls all wore little blue dresses with white caps and aprons. They did the most beautiful ironing I have ever seen. We have funny irons here. They are great big fellows with an empty space inside. You put in red-hot coals from the stove and wait until they heat the iron. They are always either too hot or too cold.

Love to all and a Merry Christmas.

December 11, 1938

Dear Family:

I feel so blue that I have to write home about it. It is all very childish, but who would not feel blue at having to work on Christmas Day! We don't think we are going to have any Christmas vacation. Every day people say, "Tomorrow the cars will run," but they never run. And as long as they do not run our students can't go home. We have been working just long enough to be ready for a vacation. Dr. Totah says, "just as soon as they start running, whether it is Christmas or April, we will have a vacation."

It is the rebels who are keeping things at a standstill. Because the British require permits for every car on the roads, the rebels won't let anybody get a permit (except American Friends Mission Schools). I don't understand all that is involved in the complication. We have several politics fiends in our school, but their discussions are all carried on in Arabic. We just have to pin them down and ask them questions when we want to know anything. Even then we don't get all the information we want.

The worst thing about Christmas is that my turn to be on duty comes on Christmas Day, so I will not get even the one-day vacation. Oh, well, there may still be a slim chance. Whether it comes in December or March, we are going to Cairo.

Gertrude and I took a walk today and found that every road except the roads to Jerusalem and Haifa have been blocked by the British. They dig a great, wide ditch right across the road and then put a stone wall across or else a mess of barbed wire. The officers have invited Gertrude and me to go up to their private cinemas every Wednesday night, but I don't think Dr. Totah will allow it, for fear it will get the schools in bad with the rebels.

Last Tuesday we teachers were reading aloud, as we often do in the evenings, and feeling so peaceful, when Bang-Bang-Bang! Rebel guns right outside the building. They had not been shooting for several weeks. The British machine guns started up soon. They were shooting across the school grounds, British on one side of the school, rebels on the other. It is the closest they have ever been. We brought all of the girls into the Teacher's room and had them sit on the floor. I sang the "Arkansas Traveler" with my teeth chattering, while the kids had to strain their ears to hear me above the guns. Then Gertrude and I sang some songs together, and Miss Widea told a funny Arabic story. The girls are good sports, and it is much easier to keep from being scared when you have to keep others calm. I just knitted and knitted because that is the most calm-appearing thing you can do. And after awhile my hands stopped shaking, and I could pick up the stitches I had dropped.

We are very fortunate in that we do not have to be afraid of raids from the air and gas. Bullets are nothing compared to what German Jews are undergoing, and to what London has been fearing all fall. Baldwin or somebody was appealing to the English people for support for the abandoned Jewish children. Compared to Europe, Palestine is a bed of roses. (But there are a good many thorns sticking out.)

Still in my gloomy mood I went down to supper and was not cheered to find sardines with the heads and scales on, salad too heavily soaked in garlic and oil and strong last year's cheese, instead of my favorite fresh white cheese. Dessert was good though, bananas (the tiny little Jericho variety), figs, and nuts. You stuff the English walnuts inside the figs, after carefully inspecting each one to see that it has no worms in it. It is perfectly good etiquette to look for worms, no worse than peeling your banana. I often find little worms preserved in the peach jam too, and it doesn't disturb me. I just push them aside. One who has eaten fried octopus on board the *Rex* can't be bothered with little things like worms.

Today I had my first real discipline problems in class. With my upper classes, where the girls are almost my own age, I never have any trouble, but with sixth-grade English, "Harame." They are a mean bunch of children, fresh from the Ramallah government school, where they have never been disciplined. I try speaking sweetly, shouting, threatening; finally I tore up the paper of one girl and made her do it over again. That produced a temporary lull. But it was Friday afternoon, and I have them for two periods. Other teachers tell me to try giving a good slap. I cannot bring myself to do that.

This was meant to be my Christmas letter, but I cannot generate much Christmas spirit. However today I was reminded of it when American mail arrived with one Christmas card for me. A gold affair from a Women's Missionary Society of Friends University, Wichita, Kansas. Never heard of any of them. Gertrude and I marveled over it. A Christmas card!

The wind is roaring around our building, which is just like an old stone fortress. Outside a cat is moaning, and farther away I hear the sound of the "wowies" (jackals). I think it is the most unearthly howl, like crazy men crying. But there is no shooting. The nights certainly vary here. Wednesday night was a full moon, and I went up on the third floor balcony to look out. The town was absolutely still. I have never seen such bright moonlight. So bright that I could even see the pink color of the roofs. It is not often you can distinguish colors by moonlight. And I could see way down the valleys. Nothing moved, no sound. Yet I knew that if I walked out on the balcony far enough to cast a shadow in the moonlight all Ramallah might be torn awake by the sound of the hidden machine guns shooting at a curfew breaker. And even after they had killed me the British would keep on shooting half the night, pretending they had something more important to shoot at when they found I was only an innocent girl.

Saturday: I just found that I have chilblains on my left hand. They come from being cold too much. Everybody gets them. They are red lumps that come on your fingers and itch and ache. They stay all winter, and your hands get more and more swollen. The old chilblains crack open and you cannot write.

Today I got my snuggies from the attic. Every time I go to my trunk, I am thrilled to see all of my lovely new underwear and things. I even have a winter dress and suit, which I haven't worn.

I'm saving them 'til after Christmas. Here's hoping that they will fit.

I am half-asleep, but must tell about the wineskins. I have seen them being carried on goat's backs. They are hideous black goatskins all puffed out with wine inside. Gertrude and I were walking slowly home after visiting Mrs. Totah at the Boys School when a Ramallah policeman came along and said, "Hurry ladies, curfew is at five o'clock this evening," so we ran all the way home and just slid over the threshold as five struck. We wondered why the change, but found out when at suppertime shooting started up. It wasn't as near as Tuesday night, but it isn't so pleasant to eat supper sitting in front of a window where a bullet may come whizzing in at any minute.

The British are using some cannon now. It makes a dull boom in the distance. I think they are using up all their oldest ammunition on our town.

One of my students, a day student here, took me for a long walk today, way down into the valley. We went to pick flowers. Since the rains, flowers have been poking up through the rocks everywhere. This is just a week before Christmas, and we picked great armloads of narcissus, daisies like some we have in our garden, smaller than our wild daisies and with many tiny long petals, tipped with rose. We also found some wild anemones, not like ours but big lavender and purple flowers that grow on furry stems. They are tougher than our variety. Then we picked maidenhair ferns in caves in the rocks. An old Arab fellow showed us where to get the sweetest narcissus. Azeeze's brother came along with some friends, boys of about sixteen. They, too, had been out spending the day in the valleys picking flowers. They gave me more armfuls of narcissus. Imagine an American boy of sixteen spending a day picking flowers. But these fellows are not afraid of being sissies. Arab boys are respected too much by their sisters and their parents to ever be sissies!

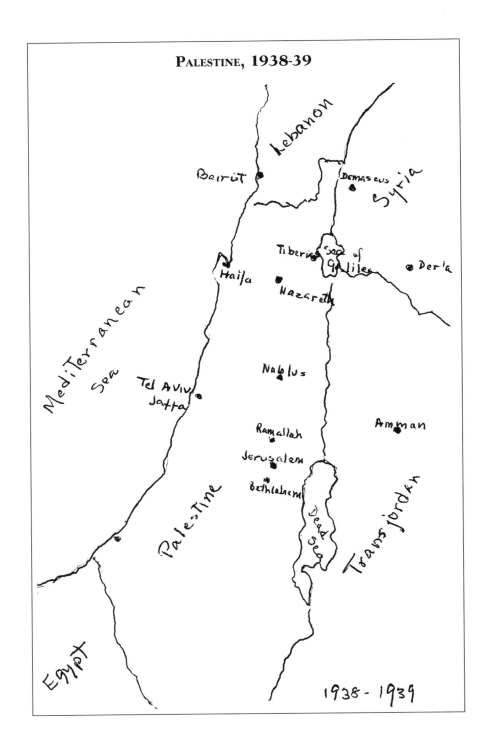

PALESTINE, 1938-39

Lebanon

Beirut

Damascus

Syria

Tiberias

Sea of Galilee

Der'a

Haifa

Nazareth

Mediterranean Sea

Nablus

Tel Aviv

Jaffa

Ramallah

Amman

Jerusalem

Bethlehem

Dead Sea

Palestine

Transjordan

Egypt

1938-1939

The valleys are so steep that you have to be careful not to fall off the edge of the cliffs. And one hill is so near the other that you can talk to the people on the next hill, even though it would take you half an hour to scramble down and up the other side.

As we walked back the sun was getting low over the hills. I came to the road that goes to Jaffa, and there I saw the "Three Wise Men" on their camels riding toward the East. They looked just like a Christmas card, which I received today!

January 10, 1939

Dear Family,

Merry Christmas. Christmas in the Holy land is still going on, with cards and letters from home arriving daily. We have three Christmases here anyway: December 25, Protestant Christmas; January 6, Greek Orthodox; and January 9, Armenian. Nice to have it spread out. The greetings, letters, and pictures from all of you have given the season the old spirit, and I wasn't too homesick. It means a lot to know that your friends and family are thinking of you when you miss them most.

In spite of the war here we sang carols and decorated the house as you did. Most of the Palestine Christians sulkily refused to celebrate, but our students said so pathetically, "We will have Christmas at school, won't we?" that we had a nice party. The teachers wrapped up small gifts for each child, the girls gave a nice play, and the glee club sang. We made a tree out of precious pine branches and had a treat of peanuts and bizer. The Boys School invited all the teachers to a *mansef* feast in honor of the new auditorium; the walls are now complete. They served a great wooden bowl of rice and meat and bread all mixed up with a very

mensaf.

rich broth. Sitting around it on the floor, we dipped in with our hands and ate with fingers.

Friday before Christmas we packed the girls off in buses and breathed deeply. Only the day before vacation transportation opened up enough for us to send the girls home. We wonder how many of the parents will send their children back. Some have already fled to Syria.

Dr. Totah said it would be impossible for us to go to Bethlehem on Christmas Eve. There had been fresh Arab uprisings and the roads were dangerous. No cars were running. However, our school driver, Salim, was willing to take the risk of the trip if the five of us paid ten piasters apiece. We went — Annice, Elmore, Roger, Gertrude and I — carrying a basket of bread and cheese for our supper. On the way, Salim insisted on stopping to show us a well where they think the three Wise Men watered their camels on the way to Bethlehem. It looked like any other well, but Roger took many pictures, one looking straight down into the water, our reflections looking back from the depths.

Bethlehem town is still medieval, yellow stone houses and narrow stone-paved streets, beautiful hills. There were few tourists on this Christmas Eve. Around the ancient Church of the Nativity military trucks were parked with sandbag walls to protect them. The door to the church is so small you have to bend over to get in. A dribbly beggar sits on a stone by the door. I think he has sat there for a thousand years, and I would not disturb his peace with the clank of a coin. But the inside of the sixteen hundred-year-old church is unmolested. You enter, stooping through a tiny door and straighten up to find yourself in a great dark basilica, long nave, flanked by rows of columns and side aisles. Way up in the apse tiny red lamps are burning. Behind the altar is a small door and a narrow stairway leading down to a chapel. It is a cave, the ceiling blackened by the smoke of many candles. A few people knelt silently near the low grotto where they believe the manger stood. Whether it is true or not, the place has certainly been made holy by the many prayers and footsteps of the faithful. The rock walls have been covered with golden tapestry, and marble slabs placed on the sacred spot. In spite of the garish decorations something of simplicity still remains in the shapeless stone walls, the worn steps, and the very quiet that lingers there. Gertrude and I sat on a rock ledge by the manger place for a long time. Four olive oil

we see the hills of Bethlehem from the church tower

lamps perpetually burning, hung over the grotto. Strange that there should be room for us to sit there on the day when the eyes of the Christian world were looking to that place. A few people came down to kiss the spot while we were there, a soldier and a priest, a blind old beggar woman and a well-dressed woman. I wished I were not a Quaker and could, with integrity, kiss the holy spot.

Outside the church we climbed the tower where we could see a lovely view of the hills where the shepherds watched their flocks. There are still shepherds there. To the east, in the distance, glittered the Dead Sea. In the North, the rounded roofs of Jerusalem gleamed across the valleys. In some damp caves under the church we stumbled over the skull of a crusader. No one goes into those catacombs any more. But Elmore and I went down to explore the crypt under the church, accompanied by a young boy,

we run accross the skull of a crusader

eager to tell us all about it in his mixture of French and Arabic.
"Here," he said, pointing to a small cell, "is where Saint Jerome
locked himself in while he was translating the Bible." We looked
so appalled at the thought of the poor saint shut into that cell for
years, probably, that the boy said cheerfully, "*Mais il est mort!*" (But,
he is dead!) What could we say? Elmore sadly shook his head and
remarked, "*Harame.*" (How sad.)

We talked to a pearl carver who called from his shop, "*Tfuddily,
tfuddily,* (Welcome)" and bought some of his mother-of-pearl stars.
He offered us wine and thick black Turkish coffee. We walked the
streets peering into the courtyards where women sit and
embroider, cook on clay charcoal-burning stoves. In the doorway of
each house a few steps lead up to a large room with a vaulted
ceiling. At the far end of this chamber are clay bins for storing
grain. Huge jugs hold the stores of water and olive oil. Woven mats
on the floor are the furniture. Directly beneath this room is a low,
cave-like room connected with the living room by stone steps.
Here are kept more supplies, the grinding mill, and the family
donkey. It was probably in such a room that Jesus was born.
Bethlehem women wear on their heads tall flower pots, covered by
white shawls. Their embroidered gowns are quite different from
the cross-stitch of Ramallah.

That evening in the
church courtyard the
soldiers had a carol
service. It seemed queer
to be singing "Peace on
Earth, Goodwill to Men"
while one soldier's
bayonet kept scratching
my shoulder. After the
carols we attended a
five-hour mass. The

The Bethlehem women

choir was pretty good, but after a few hours plainsong gets monotonous. At midnight things picked up. The music became more rhythmical; a wonderful procession of priests came in thumping their golden staffs with the beat of the music, swinging censers of incense and singing loudly. Suddenly a statue of The Child was unveiled over the altar. The mass ended at two a.m., when they carried the babe down to the grotto and put him in the manger.

We had no idea how to get home, and there is not only no room in the Inn at Bethlehem, there is no inn. "Lookin' for a way to go home?" Some soldiers of the Yorkshire regiment, stationed at Ramallah, had recognized us and offered us a ride in their open truck with machine gun mounted on top. What a way to go home on Christmas Eve. Several times on the way they stopped and shot their machine gun in all directions just in case there might be snipers hiding in the hills. I suppose they really did it to show off for the women. They almost never see English-speaking women, especially young ones.

Christmas Day dinner at Totah's: we sang and danced the Virginia reel and, since there was no curfew on Christmas, we went up and serenaded the soldiers, standing outside the electrified wire, which surrounds the barracks. The poor lads were quite drunk. I would get drunk too, if I had to be a soldier. Annice, Garnet, Gertrude and I went home to the Girls School alone, the first time I had been on the streets of Ramallah at night, after all those months of curfew.

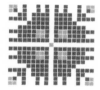

Cairo

January 12, 1939

Dear Mary,

      Remember all those years we used to pretend we were climbing the Great Pyramid, as we scrambled around the rocky ledges-at the farm? Well I have actually done it. The day after Christmas we set out for Cairo, Gertrude and I, Roger, and Elmore. In the third-class compartment of the train there are ordinary wicker seats for men, but G. and I had a *"hareem"* (train compartment) all to ourselves. At Gaza some of our students of the Boys School came to the train and brought us two huge baskets of oranges, more than we could ever carry into Egypt. The school had given us lunches to eat on the train. We slept a lot and when I woke up, we were coming out of the hills of Palestine onto the green coastal plains, planted with fragrant orange groves.

      At seven o'clock we reached Kantarra on the Suez Canal. We managed to get all the oranges that were left into one basket, which added to our burden. After paying the customs duty we found they had to be fumigated. Our luggage and our persons were carefully inspected before we took the little ferry across the

We arrive in Cairo, trying to smile

canal just in time to catch the train to Cairo. On this train there were no nice compartments for ladies, just wooden benches with drunken Egyptians who spit on the floor. Tired, hungry and too dirty to eat, we slept. It was midnight when we arrived in Cairo. Fending off the porters, the four of us found a carriage and climbed in, with suitcases, lunch bag, oranges, coats. The driver cracked his whip nobly and we clattered through the midnight streets of Cairo. It is indeed a city of mystery. We were enveloped in its weird charm that first midnight. Strange Oriental music echoed through the streets.

The Montreuse Palace, an Arab hotel someone had vaguely recommended to us, turned out to be strangely situated over a coffee shop. Despite the shifty-eyed clerk and the white-robed porter, a deaf-mute I believe, we slept pretty well and the next day looked up Manchester, our friend of the *Rex*, now a student at the American University of Cairo. He took us by streetcar out to Gizeh, where are the Pyramids and a hotel and a few grass huts for guides. The Pyramids are just as magnificent as I thought they would be. Many people said they would be disappointing, but some people make a practice of being disappointed in things, and I haven't been yet. They are just as big and solid and rugged as a mountain. The Sphinx seemed small beside them, but what nobility in her pose. We didn't look at her nearly long enough to understand her strange fascination. Some say Napoleon took off the Sphinx's nose because he didn't want anyone to have a bigger

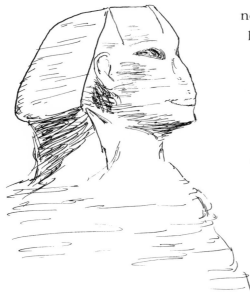

nose than he had. Others say his soldiers used her for target practice. The Sphinx has been entirely uncovered now, even to the tail. Modern Egyptians are making extensive excavations around the Pyramids and have found a whole village where the workers lived while they were building.

We walked around the three pyramids and then went into the "Great Pyramid," stooping low as we entered the narrow shaft. King Cheops, or Khufu, was buried in the exact center of the pyramid, placed in a big echoey room whose ceiling is built of granite stones fifteen or twenty feet long. There are many mysterious theories of strange mathematical formulas and forgotten architectural phenomena used in building the pyramids. Some find in them symbols which prophesy all future events of history. Astronomy books have been based on observations of the pyramids, religious enlightenment found in them. Roger took a picture of me in the empty sarcophagus of King Cheops.

To climb the pyramid you pay two piasters. They let us go without a guide, but we had to sign a paper saying, "I climb at my own risk, and I climb alone." It was a stiff ascent. The stones are about as high as my hip, some a lot higher; we had to hunt around for a way up. We climbed up the corner; the middle is too steep. Even so we found it best not to look down; it looked as if we had come up a straight wall. It feels a lot higher than the four

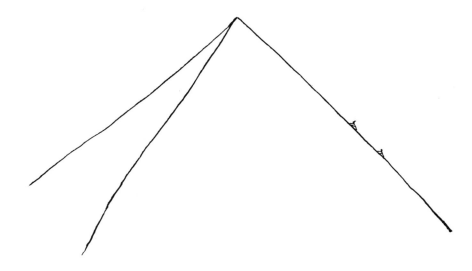

we climb a pyramid.

hundred fifty feet. On top we could see way out on the desert, a rolling sea of sand, gray and yellow. On the other side we could see clear across the Nile valley, green and fertile where it had been irrigated.

Cairo is just as Cairo should be, old and modern, gay and Oriental. Sometimes we think we are in an American city, but it couldn't be, with vendors selling everything on the streets, incense, roast chestnuts, bread, shoes etc. Most of the men wear long white night gowns, some of the richer ones wear red satin. Some wear suits, but all men wear the red *tarbusche* on their heads and don't take them off even in coffee shops, restaurants, and theaters. At night the streets ring with Oriental music. Donkey carts, hand carts, ox carts, camels, and automobiles crowd the narrow passages. Egyptians are slow, patient people who can sit for days in front of their shops, though no customers come. Some shops are devoted entirely to cleaning peoples' *tarbusche*. One shop I saw sold nothing but rosin. The men spend four or five hours each day sitting in the coffee shop talking and smoking their "*Nargeeleh*" (water pipes). Very few women go out on the streets.

One morning Gertrude and I were awakened by great excitement outside. From our balcony we could see groups of schoolboys marching by, shouting, and carts sprinkling the streets with sand, soldiers standing at attention. The king was coming! He rode in an open carriage, driven by spotless footmen. He rode as a king should, with folded arms, white gloves, and shining uniform. In another carriage came the queen and the baby in a third. The people all shouted "Farouk! Farouk!"

Love, Nance

> *Since I climbed the Great Pyramids in 1938, there has been a lively resurgence of study of its history and mystery. Archeologists from all over the world have been hacking away at the Giza monuments. The Egyptian government, realizing the significance of its most precious treasures, has established a Director*

General of the Giza Monuments to whom you must apply if you wish to do research. Tourists are still allowed to enter the king's chamber, but none are permitted to climb. The exterior limestone is beginning to crumble under too much traffic.

Some of the recent research indicates that the Sphinx and pyramids may be of much greater age than the historically accepted era of 3000 to 2600 B.C.E. Archaeologists, geologists, and astronomers all have theories of the purpose and seemingly impossible technical difficulties of building the pyramids. It does seem that those prehistoric people were acquainted with the precession of the equinox, the circumference of the earth, and many other data that we have assumed were only known since the days of classical Greece.

The research of Graham Hancock, Robert Bauval, Mark Lehman, and others points to the possibility that there could have been a highly sophisticated civilization before 15,000 years ago and that they built the monuments not for tombs but for astronomic observation or other rites. But how did they do it?

My guess is as good as anybody's. I believe the priests figured out a way of levitating those megaliths by using certain sound waves. I have tried it myself, without success.

Journal excerpts
December 29, 1938
The Valley of Kings, Egypt

We have been told that one could take a weekend excursion trip up the Nile to Luxor on a special train, all for only two pounds. Usually Gertrude and I scorn guided tours, but this seems worthwhile. It provides transportation two hundred miles up the Nile, three nights' sleeping accommodation on the train, and meals for the whole time, permits to enter the antiquities with guides, all for only ten dollars.

Elmore has been taken quite ill, fevered and weak, unable to eat. We called a doctor, who could not diagnose his trouble. Gertrude and I think it is from eating bad food. We made tea for him on a small alcohol stove I brought along from my science classroom. We tried to make porridge, the only thing we know how to cook. We held a family consultation in Manchester's room at the American University. Our happy-go-lucky Manchester, who thinks Elmore ought to accompany us to Luxor, sick or well, flopped on the floor with a pencil and paper. "Look," he said, "we'll make a chart of all the reasons for and against his going." Here is his chart.

Pro. (going to Luxor)	Con. (going to Luxor)
1. 3 days and nights of good associates and attention.	1. 3 days and nights of no association or attention.
2. Opportunity for seeing famous places.	2. No opportunity for seeing famous places.
3. Might get worse.	3. Might get worse anyway.
4. On the other hand might get better.	4. Yes.
5. Desert air.	5. Desert air.
6. $10 worth of interesting phenomena.	6. Might waste $10
7. See only Cairo.	7. See Luxor

At this, Elmore grew more ill and we will have to leave him in Manchester's room at the American University with a friend of Manchester's to care for him.

January 10, 1939
Cairo

The excursion train left Cairo about eight in the evening, packed full of good-natured, French-speaking people, and British officers. G. and I found our compartment, which was the last available on that train, really belonged to the Abyssinian porter, but he had kindly relinquished his claim for us. We had two narrow, wooden berths covered with straw mattresses, each provided with a thin red blanket. There was room beside the berths for one at a time to dress. We also had a closet, but it was full of cabbages. Under the lower berth the porter kept a bottle of whiskey. It must have been quite a necessity, for often during the chilly nights the door of our compartment would quietly slide back while a black hand reached in for the bottle of whiskey.

That first night on the train I really didn't feel like going to bed. It was New Year's Eve. Manchester and I stood out on the open platforms between the coaches earnestly exchanging philosophies between gusts of train smoke. To see the silver Nile reflecting white mountains of sand that turn to dark vegetation as they meet the waters was worth spending a New Year's Eve on that windy open platform swallowing the blowing sand and soot. Sometimes, when our train stopped at stations to take mail, we would hop off the train, daringly wait until it had started again, indeed, until it had almost passed, before we swung onto one of the last cars.

On the Train from Cairo to Luxor
Jan 1, 1939

Arriving at Luxor on New Year's morning, we left our things on the train, which was our hotel during the three days of the excursion. I was weak from not eating, and from being cold all night under the porter's red blanket. On long tables set up in the station yard like a church supper, we were served a breakfast of eggs, bread and tea. I revived a little, but still needed a square meal.

There were over a hundred people on the excursion. We were divided into smaller groups according to whether we spoke English, French, or Arabic. Driven in horse carriages, our group went first to the stupendous temple of Karnak. In the hall of columns, ninety of them, standing close together like a giant forest, one feels like a tiny beetle. The walls of everything are covered with hieroglyphic inscriptions and pictures of the kings performing their various rituals, or slaying the enemy from their speeding war chariots. How could human beings build such colossal things? There are statues of Rameses II so huge that I come up to the toe, and they are all made of one piece of rock, as are the obelisks. It seems the more important the king, the bigger and more numerous were the statues he had made of himself. Most of the sculptures around Luxor are of Ramses II.

Back at Luxor we finally had a real dinner, only I couldn't eat much trying to talk French to two priest-missionaries. In the afternoon we went to the Luxor temple, more of the stupefying statues and columns. Then some of us went for a boat ride in a typical Nile sailboat. The boatsman dipped his can into the river and drank of its magical waters. We did not accept his offer. We sang all the songs we could think of in English, French, and American.

Luxor is a typical Egyptian town. The old houses are built of mud brick mixed with straw and baked in the sun. It never rains there. They frequently sprinkle the sandy streets to make it mud. Everywhere one goes one is followed by people trying to sell things or children holding out their hands for *"baksheesh."* Upper Egypt is a flat, fertile valley between barren mountains. It is lovely to see the graceful palm trees, the Nile, and the bleak cliffs beyond.

Gertrude and I had quite a following of men, about ten English officers from the Royal Air Force and a number of men of all nations, including the chief of police in Cairo, and, of course, the faithful Roger, and Manchester, who is like a brother to us. After supper the chief of police, Mustafa, who had taken a great liking to me, asked me if I would like to have a moonlight sail on the Nile, and seeing that I was delighted with the Egyptian musicians, he even hired a whole orchestra to come along and play for me. I asked Mustafa if he minded my bringing along a few friends. He looked a bit crestfallen and said I must do whatever would please me. So I invited Gertrude, Roger and Manchester, the two Maltese lads, and a few of the Englishmen. Poor Mustafa. It was a lovely sail. The musicians played clay drums and reed flutes that made the Nile a fairy river. They did queer dances with their strange music.

After the sail, we walked the streets eating sugar cane. On the station platform we did the Lambeth Walk and the Virginia Reel and some English dances. We sang until we were sleepy, then tried to explore the temple by night, but it was too heavily guarded.

The next day early in the morning we took boats across the Nile. Open automobiles drove us seven miles over dusty desert roads into the Valley of Kings. We passed the two Colossi of Memnon, seated statues that guard the valley where the ancient Kings were buried; sixty-one have been found and they know there are three which have not yet been unearthed. These tombs date back to about 2000 B.C. (the pyramids, 3300).

We went first to the tomb of Tutankamen, the only tomb that has been found unrobbed (though molested by grave robbers who must have been frightened away). It is the smallest of all the tombs, because he was an unimportant king and he died young. Most of its contents have been taken to the Cairo Museum. We had seen them there: furniture made of wood covered with gold, jewels, clothes, food and hundreds of golden images and containers. The body itself was encased in three gold coffins, each a figure of the king, and placed in three gold sarcophagi. In the actual tomb of Tutankamen, they have kept the inner stone sarcophagus and the innermost gold coffin containing the mummy. And there he has lain, staring at the painted ceiling these three thousand years.

Tutankamen was the son of Iknaton, a king who tried to introduce monotheism into Egypt about 1200 B.C. Because he believed in one sun god, Aton, he changed his name from Amenhotep to Iknaton, the son of Aton. He established a new capital of Egypt at Amarna and called his little son Tutankaton, after the great sun god. However, Iknaton died when his heir was too young to rule and his faithless ministers immediately brought back the old polytheistic religion, calling the child king Tutankamen.

The larger tombs are great chambers cut out of rock underground. The walls are covered with hieroglyphics and pictures, painted in bright colors. Some rooms were for sacrificing, some for storing food and furniture. The greatest chamber was for the sealed sarcophagus. They sometimes made false chambers so that robbers would think the tomb had already been robbed. No modern institution has equaled these giant undertakings for size, durability, and elaborateness of decoration. If you have time to study the wall paintings you can learn a great deal about life in ancient Egypt. We visited the tombs of Seti, Ramses III, and Tutankamen. In the afternoon we took a long donkey ride out into the country: palm groves, mud villages, irrigated fields, and orange groves, where we picked oranges and tangerines. On the way back we had a donkey race along the main highway.

That night we again slept on the train, which remained in Luxor station. In the morning I was awakened by a great commotion. Since we had to perform our ablutions in the station wash room, I slipped on my bathrobe, snatched my towel and toothbrush, and jumped off the train. As I did so, the shouting increased and I soon discovered it was directed at me. A luxurious red Persian carpet had been spread over the station platform and I seemed to be the only person standing on it. Soldiers, standing at attention, were stationed around it while I stood alone in bathrobe and pajamas clutching my toothbrush. The train from which I had descended had moved away behind me and another train was steaming into the station.

With everyone shouting at me in Arabic I hardly knew what to do. Finally I realized this was the Sultana's private carpet laid out to welcome her to Luxor. Gathering up the shreds of my dignity, I slipped between the soldiers and joined the crowd, just in time to see the Sultana, mother of King Farouk, step off her train. A military band struck up the national anthem, the Sultana nodded to left and right, the crowd cheered, and I snuck into the station wash room to wait for my own train to return.

I stand on the Sultana's carpet.

Back in Cairo, we found poor Elmore no better. He looked very hollow-eyed and yellow, and we began to wonder how we would get him back to Palestine. We fixed him tea. The doctor still didn't know what was the matter (later we found it was hepatitis). We gave him another day to rest before the return trip. Our two English officers, Reg and Ken, remained very attentive to Gertrude and me. They took us to stylish places to eat and sightseeing at all the mosques we had missed the week before. On our last night in Egypt they hired a special car with chauffeur and drove us out to see the pyramids by moonlight. Now the pyramids by moonlight are extremely romantic and when I see something romantic I'd rather not talk. But an Englishman likes to deliver an oration of the great thoughts that arise in him. So Ken voiced all the deep and strange ideas that the Sphinx suggested. Coming home in the car we sang. Ken squeezed my hand tiresomely. Englishmen are too obvious, Arabs too subtle, and Americans too clumsy. What is a poor girl to do?

When we left Cairo, Reg and Ken and Manchester came to see us off on the train. Elmore was barely able to stagger into the third-class carriage with all the peasants. I felt especially sorry to leave dear old Manchester. Who knows if we will ever see him again? As the train pulled out, I looked back, wistfully waving until Manchester was just a little speck, tossing up his hat. A week later I had a letter from Ken, the Englishman. He had, he said, fallen in love with me and he felt sure there was some answering glimmer in my eye, for, "when the train pulled out of the station in Cairo, you looked back so sadly."

At Kantarra, on the Suez Canal, officials told us the Palestine train would not start until daylight because it was dangerous to travel through rebel territory at night. Gertrude and I roamed around the dusty desert town all night. Ladies couldn't go into the coffee house where Roger  and Elmore sat drinking strong tea. Walking back over the moonlit sands we saw a big freighter ship moving out in the middle of the broad desert. It was in the unseen waters of the Suez Canal.

Winter, 1939

Mid-January, 1939

All the students have come back after the Christmas vacation. Now that I've had some experience, I feel more confident about teaching. We spend our free time trying to get warm; feet are always cold from standing on the stone floors of the classroom. Weather is rainy, with chilling east winds. Running short of olive wood, we do not light the little stove in the teachers' room, have to save all the wood for cooking. Yesterday G and I found a *canoon* (native clay stove); the cook gave us a few hot coals from the kitchen stove, and we sat cozily with it in our room until we began to feel drowsy. Remembering that burning coals give off gas, I opened the window. No more *canoon*, just get in bed with hot water bottle.

It rains and rains. In the "new building" where I teach most of my classes, the roof leaks, the windows leak, and I stand in a puddle most of the day. We wear wool skirts and sweaters and winter coats, but the Arab teachers wear silk dresses. We teachers are about the only women in Ramallah who do not wear the native dress. I wonder what the women wear under those gowns of hand-woven linen, elaborately embroidered. Students wear wool uniforms with hand-knitted sweaters and, in the cold classroom, coats and mittens (to keep away the chillblain); the wealthy girls have warm furry goatskins under their feet.

Science is my best class, but when it came to dissecting a toad, the girls would not let me kill it because it is holy. I was greatly relieved — never did like dissecting. They were amazed when they learned about sex. The teachers later told me they are not supposed to know about that until they marry. None of our teachers are married. How did they know?

I am not so strong in history, studied very little of that in college, but I manage to keep ahead. After all they are studying in a foreign language. Those of our students who go on to University of Beirut do quite well, but if our girls went to an American college they would have to take one or two years of high school before they could get in. Very few go on to college. Most women in Palestine are illiterate. When we buy eggs and bread from Ramallah women, we have to take a thumbprint instead of a signature on their bill receipts. And some of these are the mothers of our students. Among our teachers, those who teach lower grades speak very little English. Table conversation is mostly in Arabic, except at the English end of the table.

January 25, 1939

The wildflowers are out in the valleys, tiny narcissus, pushing up exquisite, noddy heads through the thorn bushes, miniature cyclamen and big, velvety anemones, purple and red. There are dainty little orchids, which they call the "bee orchid." Since the Arab agitation has calmed down a bit, the staff feels it is safe

enough to take a few short trips into the valleys for wildflowers.
Picking flowers is a favorite recreation in Palestine for both men
and women. The valleys are steep and rocky. I long to investigate
the many caves, but it is said that rebels hide there. When the
rain lets up, we leap from rock to rock shouting and singing. With
nobody around for miles, our voices echo down the valleys,
scaring the jackals in their caves. Their howling is rather bone
chilling. Wherever there is a flat space olive trees grow. Since the
rains, the barren hills are turning green where wheat is planted
on some of the hillsides, but it grows sparsely. If a plane flies over
we must stand perfectly still. They are said to drop bombs on
anything they see moving in the valleys.

February 15, 1939

 Things are easing up. They have put back the telephones and
post office in Ramallah. We don't have to wait hopefully for
someone to go to Jerusalem for the
mail. Curfew is put off to nine
o'clock. Cars can go without
being stopped every mile to
show your passport or permit,
without always keeping alert for
armed soldiers, rebels, or land
mines, being advised to go back.
We still have shooting every
night, but the London conference
between Arabs and Jews has
accomplished one thing. The two Arab
parties have joined together so that we

have only three groups at sword point instead of four. The Ramallah soldiers have been commanded not to use their machine guns so freely. They are doing too much damage, making holes in people's houses, shooting cats and donkeys or anything they see moving at night. They are ordered to use rifles instead. We still study on the cold floor at night, but no bullets have yet come through our windows. In the evenings we English-speaking teachers sometimes sit in the teachers parlor, while Annice reads to us: *Rebecca* by Daphne Dumaurier, *The Yearling* by Marjorie Rawlings.

When I was on duty last night, we had an extra amount of shooting. The little girls are always afraid when there is shooting, in fact, everybody has a queer feeling in their stomach. The little girls trailed around after me, and I remembered when I was little following Mother around during thunderstorms. After I put the little ones to bed, the older students told me some girls were over in the classroom building afraid to come back because of the shooting. This was a time when the job calls for heroic acts, and you don't feel at all heroic. But the girls must not stay out there all night.

I ran. Although the building is only a few hundred feet from the main dormitory, it seemed miles away. The shooting went on at intervals and the girls sat on the steps crying, thoroughly frightened. Finally when it died down a bit, I turned out all the lights in the classroom building, made the children hold hands and dash for home. Halfway back a new round of shooting started up quite close. Effit, the youngest girl, gave a shriek and fell to the ground. "I'm shot, I'm shot." I told the others to go on and they ran home crying, "Effit is dead, Effit is dead!" Effit was not dead, not even hurt, only foolishly frightened. "Get up, Effit." I said. She sobbed and rolled over. The shooting continued. I shook her and up she jumped, more afraid of me than the bullets. After all, if she were hurt, her cries would have been in Arabic.

How to Make *Taboon* Bread:

First you grow the wheat, plowing your rocky plot of ground with your wooden plow and donkey. In midwinter, sow the precious seed and pray to Allah for rain. The wheat grows sparsely among the stones, but if the young shoots are not washed away in a downpour, or dried up in the sun; if the jackals don't run them down, or British soldiers trample them, or rebels steal the ripe wheat, harvest it, using your sickle to cut and your wife to carry the bound sheaves home on her head. What she can't carry you load onto a camel. You ride home on the donkey. Save the straw to be woven into mats. Take the wheat to the threshing ground and trample it barefoot until the sweet grains are loosened from their hulls. Then on a windy day, take a pitchfork and toss the wheat into the breeze. The chaff blows away and the good wheat drops to the ground. "The ungodly are not so; but are like the chaff which the wind driveth away." (Psalms 1:4). After many days of threshing the wheat is ready to be sorted. And from here on the wife takes over. On flat woven trays she sorts the seeds, picking out the black "tares," then takes it to the mill for grinding.

To make the *taboon* bread: first build a small, round, stone house, having one door and no windows. In the center of the stone house put a bed of ashes. Then make out of clay a very big jar and lid and bury it in the ashes. This is the oven, or *taboon*. In the bottom of the *taboon*-jar place red-hot coals, cover them with clean stones and spread over the stones round flat loaves of raised dough. Place a lid on the jar and cover completely with ashes. Sit in the warm stone house with friends, singing for one hour. Remove the bread from the *taboon* and shake out the stones. Eat while deliciously warm and soft. It is best when dipped in fresh olive oil and sprinkled with *zattar*, a ground herb.

Making Olive Oil:

After you harvest the olives they are not fit to eat until they have soaked in salt water a year. Fresh olives are bitter. But they can be used for oil. The oil press is a community enterprise. Like a wine press it works by screwing a board down on the olives. Lay them under the press in a burlap bag. Pour boiling water over the bag of olives to loosen the oil, and collect the oil and water in a tub below the press. A lady with beautiful hands scoops the floating oil from the water and drops it into your jar. Use this oil in nearly everything you cook and dip the bread in a little oil for breakfast.

A *Tabbouli* Party:

When the grape leaves are young and tender invite your friends to a *tabbouli* party. In a large wooden bowl mix *borghul*, olive oil, chopped parsley, onions, and lemon juice. Pass the grape leaves and each guest scoops up the *tabbouli* from the bowl with a grape leaf. Sing this song.

Tabboulit na maki la ha	Tabboulit how nice it is,
Tabboulit na ahala ha	Tabboulit how good it is,
Tabboulit ha tabboulit	Tabboulit, oh tabboulit.
Shoo ful bourgel, shoo ful zeit,	Made of wheat and
Shoo ful zeit.	olive oil.
Kulu min ha dir il beit,	All things grown at
Min il beit	our own home.
B'eedee anna majboolit,	And mixed by my own hands
Ha tabboulit, ha tabboulit.	Tabboulit, oh tabboulit.

You can also play *tabbouli* games, where you slip the grape leaf out of somebody's hand, just as he is about to take a bite. This causes merry shouts of laughter and smeared faces. After *tabbouli*, which is usually served out in the apricot orchard, pick all the ripe mish-mish (apricots) you can eat. The seeds are good too, cracked open and eaten fresh.

February 21, 1939

Dear Mother,

There's not so much shooting now. We have been to Jerusalem several times, for shopping, dentist, and once Kareemeh Nassir, her brother, and two of his friends took us dancing at the King David Hotel. Last weekend Gertrude, Kareemeh, and I spent the weekend in Jerusalem. We visited the Old City. The officer at Jaffa gate said, "You can go in without much danger, but don't go down David street," and listed a lot of other streets we mustn't go to. However, we did see David's citadel, a famous landmark, so old that nobody knows when it was built. They think Solomon started it, and every king who came along added another wall so that now the walls are about thirty feet thick. It was used by the Turks twenty years ago, and is now being used by the British. It seemed only right to see guns and bayonets piled inside the citadel, even modern gas masks didn't appear to be out of keeping with the old fortress, for it has always been adapted to the latest kind of warfare. They are also doing excavations to see if they can find the beginning of the fortress. There are deep holes full of water, places where people have kept olive oil, and tunnels that go all under the city. It was raining hard all afternoon. We were the only people in the citadel, except for a few bedraggled soldiers.

Back at our hotel (The Majestic) we changed to dry things and then Labeeb Nassir and Sameh and Najeeb took us out to supper in a charming German restaurant. The school had asked us not to go to the King David Hotel for dancing any more, too Jewish, even though our Arab friends like to go there. We did see our Jewish friend from the *Esperia*, but could not talk very much because of the coldness of our Arab friends when we introduced him. Hard to be consistent when you are an Arab, but we were their guests.

They always plan the nicest surprises for us. Sunday we met the conductor of the Jerusalem Symphony Orchestra, a baritone of the YMCA glee club, and an excellent organist who played for us on the YMCA organ while the baritone sang. Afterwards we all went to the baritone's house and sang some more, met his relatives and drank Turkish coffee — thick, sweet and black. Then to dinner at the YMCA and a drive out toward Jaffa through some interesting hills. Looking down over the Mediterranean we could see a large boat, anchored a few miles off shore. It was crowded with people on the deck in the hot sun. Labeeb told us they were Jewish refugees, escaping from Hitler's Germany, not allowed to land in Palestine. Where could they go? We never heard what became of them.

We came back to tea and a concert and reception for some Americans. Then to the cinema and then to the home of some friends of Kareemeh's. A very lovely modern house all decorated in black and white, from the ebony piano to the calla lilies on the low table, quite a contrast to the usual red overstuffed furniture and cushions we see in Ramallah homes.

Well, back to the classroom now.

Love,

Nance

March 20, 1939

Dear Family,

Gertrude and I felt our weekend in Jerusalem, being entertained by Kareemeh and her friends was not entirely satisfying. They gave us the best American-type entertainment Jerusalem could offer. But we were anxious to see the Oriental and historic side of the city. Secretly we planned a weekend all by ourselves. We took a bus early Saturday morning before breakfast.

As Damascus gate is only open from six to eight in the morning, we hurried into the old city and explored until the British soldiers chased us out. Then we went to the section of the Orthodox Jews and saw the wailing wall and the outside of the wonderful mosque, "Haram Es Sherif" (Dome of The Rock). The Mosque is built over the rock from which Mohammed ascended into heaven. His footprint is still there. It was inconsiderate of Mohammed to use this rock for his takeoff, because it is the same

rock on which Abraham was about to sacrifice Isaac, and also the site of the holy temple of Solomon. The rock is pitted with channels and holes and has probably been used as a sacrificial rock since prehistoric times. But now it is holy to both Jews and Moslems, and their separate claims are the cause of much bitterness. At the wall the Orthodox Jews really wail. You can hear their voices from afar. They take their bibles, read portions of Lamentations, and chant mournful songs in unison with the rabbis. Their faces are streaked with tears.

We went to a Jewish restaurant for lunch and there we saw an English chap whom we had met in our earlier travels. He teaches at St. George's School in Jerusalem and invited us to a cricket match and to tea. The "masters" were playing the English military. We sat with some rather tough English women, wives of officers. The game was interminable. There was an interlude for tea and then more cricket. We excused ourselves about five. Gertrude had a bad infection in her foot and could hardly walk. Back at the hotel, who should turn up but Labeeb Nassir; how he found out we were in Jerusalem we never knew. But he took us out to dinner and the cinema and afterwards to the inevitable cafe, where you sit and drink warm lemonade and listen to a bad imitation of American Jazz.

The next morning, since Gertrude didn't want to walk, I got up early and made a pilgrimage all around the walls of the Old City. On the west side is the oldest church in the world, mostly underground. The entrance is a black hole in a low wall, and about a hundred steps lead down into a pitch-dark cavern. From below I could hear the wavering strains of voices chanting the Greek Orthodox mass. I felt my way down to the chapel where a few candles lit the icons. When I stepped into a dark corner my groping hand felt the greasy beard of a black robed priest. The nuns near the altar were singing the strange harmony that the Greek Orthodox use. This church supposedly houses the tombs of

St. Mary, St. Joseph, and St. Anne.

From the church of St. Anne I went to the garden of Gethsemene, where some olive trees that were there in the time of Christ grow. Olive oil from these trees sells at a high price. Way up the hill is a Russian Church. Their nuns wear tall, pointed hats. The choir sings all out of

tune. Since no one ever sits down in a Russian church, I did not stay long at Mass. In the Valley of Kidron, I scrambled over square tombstones in the ancient Jewish cemetery. There were the towering tombs of Absolam and Zacharias. Down a little dirt road, some Arab women told me to go back, but I didn't, which was very unwise. I climbed a steep path leading around the east corner of the old city wall and found on the hillside Arab men harvesting wheat. The path was narrow in places, and there was only a ledge between the wall and a steep drop down into the valley. Some peasant women coming down the path toward me shook their fists and shouted. They looked so mean and were coming upon me so fast I thought they were going to shove me off the cliff. I couldn't call to them when they were all talking at once, so I looked across the valley at the Greek church and crossed myself in the Orthodox way. Then they knew I wasn't a Jew and let me go by. I finished my pilgrimage hastily, bought some food for our breakfast, and went back to the hotel, where I found Gertrude not much better.

At 9:30 Labeeb came and took us to the Mosque. He had all the necessary passes and permits for us to go and brought a car and four men to escort us. One of the men was very knowledgeable, a guide with both intelligence and influence. I don't know why these Arab men are so nice to *us*. Labeeb always arranges things easily and then pays all the bills as if it were a privilege. To go to the mosque, you have to go a long way through the old city. Of course you can't take a car into the old city, none of the gates are wide enough, and the streets are too narrow. The escorts were glad to help Gertrude walk on her painful foot. We entered through Damascus gate and followed the "via Dolorosa," stopping at the "stations" now pictured in every Catholic church. Many of the narrow streets are shaded by stone arches, a great relief from the hot sun. The Mosque of Omar (Dome of the Rock, or Harem es Sherif) is a six-sided temple with a huge, graceful dome. Every inch of the walls is covered with bright Jerusalem tiles, beautifully glazed and painted. Inside, the walls are faced with marble, laid so that the streaks make patterns. The ceiling is finely mosaiked in gold and rich colors, with the words of the Koran written in gold all over the upper walls. We met the caretaker of the temple, a most respectable old fellow who has inherited his right to the job for over five hundred years. He told us how the Koran says the Jews will never become a nation. Under the temple area there is a great underground room all braced with ancient columns. This was the base of Solomon's temple, and the area was used to stable his horses. From these chambers passages lead way beneath the city, most of them now blocked off.

Back home we had to put Gertrude to bed. Her foot had a huge blister on the bottom and she was running a little fever. It's a ringworm infection. I am the only one allowed to take care of her, and I have to disinfect myself, hands, feet etc, every day. Our room is cleaned with Lysol. Enough for now.

Love,

Nance

Journal Entry
March 17, 1939
More Politics

The conference in London, between British, Arabs, and Jews has been going on all winter. Nashejeebeh, the unpopular Arab who favors cooperation with the British, is there and the Mufti, from hiding in some European country, suddenly appeared wearing his best turban. At first the conference didn't go very well. The Arabs had religious scruples about sitting in the same room with Jews. Now, after months of dispute and false rumors, the British have issued their decision, The White Paper. The provisions of The White Paper are:

1. Give the Palestinians independence in ten years, gradually letting Arabs and Jews take over offices as heads of departments.
2. Immigration: Allow Jews to come in for five years, until they reach one third of the total population.
3. Arabs and Jews will rule jointly, dividing government offices between them.
4. No more Arab land must be sold to Jews. The High Commissioner will take charge of sale of property.

As a result of the White Paper, the Arabs stopped attacking the British and the Jews started. More bombs went off in Jerusalem every day. The Jews burned the government offices that hold the records of immigration. They are not satisfied with a minority. They are bombing government buildings and market places where Arabs frequently gather. They threw four bombs at Jaffa gate, the busiest spot in Jerusalem. I don't see why everybody took the

White Paper so seriously, promising Palestine independence after ten years. Who ever heard of Great Britain's keeping a promise for ten years?

> *It has been sixty-two years since that White Paper. The British have lost their mandate and their empire. The Jews have become a nation, Israel, strong and aggressive. They have taken away much of the Arab's homeland and their rights to be citizens of their own country: to have a passport, to travel, to use un-rationed water of their own (while Israelis use the water for their swimming pools and lawns).*

Syria and Transjordania

April 1, 1939, Ramallah

Dear Folks,

Gertrude and I have decided to take our spring vacation trip by ourselves, without Roger and Elmore. We have found that two women alone can go places more easily without men along. We decided to go to Amman, then Damascus, Baalbek, and Beirut. But we have no idea how to get to these places, now that public transportation is so unreliable. Well, wait for report in two weeks.

April 23, 1939

We went to the British police and hitchhiked by armored car to Jerusalem. At the barracks in Jerusalem (The Citadel of David), the first thing we saw was Roger and Elmore sitting on a pile of planks and looking very dejected. They were hoping to hitch a ride by convoy to Amman. Nope, said the soldiers, roads are too dangerous between here and Jericho. There are no trains or buses running now. While we were sitting forlornly on our suitcases by

Jaffa gate, our British police friends came along. "What? Haven't you gone yet?" Then they said they were going to Haifa that afternoon and would take us in the armored car. Roger and Elmore said they would come along with us. Here we were, sharing our luck and giving them a free ride all the way to Haifa.

An armored car isn't as safe as it sounds. The sides are bulletproof, but the floors are made of wood. What if we hit a land mine? There are tiny, slit windows for the drivers and small holes for guns, otherwise you can't see out. Our driver amused us by telling us how he had been shot while driving, and how bullets could come right through the window. At each village he would say, "This is one of the worst towns in the country. Last week they ... etc." We begged them to take their guns out so we could see through the holes.

The eastern hills of Palestine are steep and wild. We went by way of Tel Aviv because Nablus is now too dangerous. When we reached the plains, we could see where the desert stops and fertility begins. Camels were peacefully grazing in green fields. Fragrant orange groves were just ready to bloom. One of the men said, "Ten years ago this was all desert." Tel Aviv is an ultramodern city of new, white houses, bright restaurants and stores, people walking around in shorts, noisy, lively, purposeful. Just the opposite of Arab villages. We stopped there for tea.

Near Haifa the mountains closed in, leaving a narrow plain next to the Mediterranean. We were laughing and singing when suddenly the men began shooting from our car. We all crouched in the bottom, but thinking they just did it to scare us, we got up and brushed ourselves off. More shooting. They said snipers were shooting at us from the hills. At Haifa we found a clean hotel in the Jewish section. The streets were brightly lit and we had ICE CREAM CONES! The next morning, escaping from Roger and Elmore, we climbed Mt. Carmel, a beautiful hill overlooking the bay. We could see far out into the Mediterranean — blue, blue, blue.

When we inquired if it was safe to go to Nazareth and Tiberius, the Jews assured us it would be safe to go by their bus. The ride to Nazareth is beautiful, through green hills dotted with grazing camels. We passed the famous communistic Jewish colonies where all the tiny houses are just alike, and that is about as close as we will get to any Jewish homes in this country. The bus had almost passed Nazareth before we realized it. Gertrude hurriedly pulled the stop bell and they left us in the middle of the road, bag and baggage, not knowing what to do or where to go. Nazareth is an Arab rebel center, hence the Jewish bus' wanting to hurry through. It's a beautiful village, nestling in the hills and abloom with churches. The oldest church, built where Jesus, Mary, and Joseph lived, is now a cave, deep underground. It was buried long ago by earthquakes and accumulation of debris. While we walked the town, a bomb exploded at the government police station. We went on to a convent and bought exquisite laces from the nuns.

No other buses ran that day, but the Sabbaghs, the family of two of our students, begged us to stay with them. They must have slept six in a bed to make room for us; there are seven children in the family. We had delicious *tabbouli*. Although the parents could not speak English, we got along pleasantly in our halting Arabic.

In the morning, Mr. Sabbagh took us to the bus station in Nazareth. It was especially good of him to walk right through the town with us who look so much like Jews. We waited and waited, but no bus came. Finally a Jewish private car came through and the driver recognized us, for he had been driving the bus we took yesterday. He stopped and invited us to go on to Tiberius with him. I noticed he was armed with a revolver under his coat, which he later took out and laid on the seat beside him. Turns out he felt safer with women in the car, because the Arabs are less likely to shoot at women.

Tiberius is by the Sea of Galilee and we were, they said, the first tourists who had entered the town for over a year. The British police, not having seen English speaking women for a long time, were delighted to scold us and tell us of all the dangers of this town and then took us to the one hotel, where we were treated as special guests. We explored the old fortress of Roman Emperor Tiberius, dabbled in the water and went out for a row on the Sea of Galilee. What peace! The blue lake, surrounded by sparkling mountains, took away all the stress of the last few days as we drifted over the pleasant waters.

The police kept a rather close eye on us, but the manager of the hotel invited us to tea and to meet some English gentlemen. With all this attention, military escorts and police protection, we felt quite set up. But elation was followed by dismay when they forbade us to continue our journey to Damascus. The nearest railroad, they said, is ten miles away at a town called Semakh, more dangerous even than Tiberius. From Semakh a railroad goes up East of Galilee through the mountains of Transjordan and Syria, rebel territory. After much persuasion, they agreed to take us, heavily guarded, to Semakh and hand us over to an immigration official, who would take care of us from then on to Damascus. They were all shocked to find that we travel third class.

On the train, East of Galilee.

This train compartment, *hareem*, is tightly packed, with us and four heavily veiled Moslem women. But whenever the door is closed, the women put up their veils and become cheerfully friendly. When the door opens a crack, down come the veils. With ticket collectors and customs and immigration officials frequently dropping in, the women are kept quite busy. The seats are hard and uncomfortable. The compartment is hot and we can't see out very well. They offer us food, which we are afraid to eat. There is a small puddle on the floor where some child has wet.

Later: We were beginning to wish we had bought second-class tickets when our caretaker, the immigration officer, invited us to occupy a first-class coach. We have a whole compartment to ourselves, soft seats and room to move. Best of all we can see out, even open the windows. We are going up, up, up through narrow green valleys, from six hundred feet below sea level into the high mountains of Syria. From great cliffs, there are spectacular waterfalls; we crossed a rushing river and now are riding a narrow ledge on an almost vertical mountainside. Wait.

Now, near the top of some barren slopes we are passing a few villages of mud houses and groups of Bedouin tents. The women run out to watch the train go by, their black dresses blowing in the wind. I threw a penny to one tiny girl — I owed it to her because she was so pretty, bundled in a black shawl.

We spent the rest of the day crossing the high plateau dotted with grazing camels. This is the spring season when grass is plentiful. Later in the summer it will dry up and the whole Bedouin community will move to higher pastures. I was intrigued by some blue flowers growing by the railroad tracks. As we stopped in a small station I called to a soldier in a strange uniform, *"Bidde Zahre Azura."*

"That's funny, he doesn't seem to know what I am saying."

"Yes, it's funny," said Gertrude, "since you speak such perfect Arabic."

"But we're in Syria, maybe he speaks French." *"Monsieur le Soldat, voulez vous me donnez une fleure bleu, s'il vous plais?"* ("Mister soldier, would you please pick me one of those blue flowers?") The soldier was delighted and picked me an armload of blue flowers.

We stopped at Deraa, on the border of Jebel Druz, mountain country of the mysterious Druz people who espouse a religion of mixed Jewish, Christian, Islamic, and pagan beliefs. The women, unveiled, with tattooed faces, wear brilliant costumes and the men wear anything they can find, but cover it all with a huge woolen cloak, hand woven, of course. On their heads they wear turbans

wound in a way peculiar to the Druz. At the station stops we
leaned from our windows to see all the strange sights, and people
crowded around to look at us. It is likely that they had never seen
a white person, and with uncovered head.

As we progressed into the high desert plain, the country
became more wild. There were tiny mud villages miles apart. This
is the region where civilization began, about 7000 B.C., and I
think it has changed very little here ever since those first people
were inspired to live in community. They farm a little, in the rainy
season, using wooden plows and irrigating with runoff melt from
the mountains. They raise wheat and lentils, camels, and goats.

Though they walk miles to their fields, they must live in
villages, because the Bedouin tribes are always at war. They are
governed by some kind of feudal system. There are no roads or
automobiles or even horses, only camels and donkeys. The narrow-
gauge railroad is their only link to civilization.

At sunset the flat stretches of plain were lovely, with
mountains in the distance. We could still see the snowcap of Mt.
Hermon. Occasionally we stopped out in the middle of space to
unload people for towns that were far away across the fields.
Toward evening the plain became a mysterious purple. It seemed
to me, leaning out of the train window, to be the most beautifully
lonely place I had ever seen. After dark not one of the Bedouin
villages had a single light. About once an hour we stopped at a
tiny station lighted by one candle. At last we saw Damascus,
twinkling against a dark mountain.

We took a carriage to Rest Haven, a homey rooming house run
by an American woman, and here we shall stay a while. Hot water,
good food. Damascus is having a strike against the French
government, but Syrians don't take their strikes as seriously as the
people of Palestine. When they discovered there were two
American women in town, they declared a holiday from their
strike. Now, every time we walk down the "Street Called Straight"

we hear the shop fronts rolling up as we approach, and goods are being moved out onto the sidewalk where most of the marketing takes place. Damascus is famous for its bazaars. There are bright silks, tinkling silver jewelry, painted leatherwork and hand-carved brasswear. I was lured into a shop by a particularly enticing shopkeeper. In the bazaar they speak all languages.

The houses, in old Damascus, have upper floors that project over the narrow streets, giving much-needed shade. Windows are covered with openwork wooden screens so that the women of the *hareem* can peek out without being seen. Every Syrian house has a courtyard and a fountain unseen from the street. Damascus is the hub of the Orient, with its water vendors, rattling brass cups, loaded donkeys, blocking every passage, and — in the dark back streets — shops where men are making inlaid furniture, carved brass, ivory combs, leatherwork, and blown glass.

We wandered about the streets for two days, visited the famous old Omayed Mosque, explored an ancient caravan inn where you enter through the "needle's eye," a tiny door cut into big iron gates, which are only opened for camels. There is a Syrian palace of the twelfth century, its ceiling still glittering with painted, gold patterns; its elaborate Turkish baths ready for some idle princess. The modern Turkish bath is a series of rooms heated to different degrees, where the bather spends a whole day passing from one steamy chamber to the next.

Our Arab hotel was depressingly shabby, but it only cost twenty-five cents a night. Food is very cheap in Damascus, but rather dirty. When we got very hungry, we ordered eggs and hot tea. The rest of the time we lived on bananas and oranges. We had to speak French and Arabic, as no one in Damascus can speak English.

On Sunday we took the train for Baalbek, a seven-hour trip. After trying several third-class compartments, we found one that wasn't too crowded. We don't like to ride with Arab women, because they are sloppy and noisy and carry many dirty babies. In our compartment were four nice old Arab men, who sat peacefully smoking their water pipes and eating their unleavened bread with sour cheese. They were hurt when we didn't partake, but they carry the food wrapped up in a dirty scarf, and spread it out on the seat. Everybody eats on the train. When you hang out the window, lettuce leaves, and orange peels fly back and hit you in the face. I think trains are the most amusing part of all our travels. But you have to be feeling pretty fit to be able to take it third class.

Baalbek is on a plain between snow-capped mountains. In America it would be made into a million-dollar, summer resort. We wanted to see the remains of the great Temple of Jupiter. It is said that the old temple has seen so many sunsets that the four remaining columns have turned pink on their western sides. To enter the famous temple cost a Syrian pound (fifty cents) so we couldn't afford supper that night. The temple is a Roman structure, dedicated to Jupiter. No modern structure can hold a candle to those colossal columns and delicate stone carvings. People today don't have time to make impressive buildings.

We had another seven-hour train journey from Baalbek to Beirut. The train was jammed, and we were so weak with hunger that we couldn't enjoy the people much, couldn't even laugh when molasses came dripping down from the baggage rack all over our sleeping neighbors. There wasn't any place in Baalbek clean enough to eat; we hadn't had solid food for more than two days. We crossed the high Lebanon Mountains and came down to the coast.

In Beirut we staggered into a restaurant near the American University, and the first person we saw was a Jewish boy whom we had known on the *Rex*. Food revived us a bit and we hunted up Jim Gidney, another friend of our voyage. He showed us all around the American University, where he teaches. It is about the best university in the Near East, except the Hebrew University at Jerusalem. Moses Bailey and his wife (New England Friends) entertained us at their home. Moses Bailey is spending a sabbatical year from Hartford Theological Seminary teaching at the American University of Beirut and studying Oriental languages. They visited us in Ramallah a few weeks before. It was fun staying in an American home again. They had a beach picnic for us on the shores of the Mediterranean where we found all sorts of queer shells and sea anemones on the rocks. The Mediterranean really is bluer than other seas and is much saltier.

The next day the Baileys took us for a trip way up in the mountains to Beit Edine to see an old Druz castle. The Lebanon Mountains are steeper and higher than the White Mountains. It is wild country, but at least it has a few dirt roads. We saw real cedars of Lebanon. I loved the little mountain towns and the bright costume of the Druz people. The roads zigzag up the mountainsides and you think you are going to slide off the road and fall down to the valley below. Our Arab driver insisted on coasting down the mountains to save petrol (which costs fifty cents a gallon here). The day was literally and figuratively the high spot in our trip. We also saw the Phoenician city of Sidon with good Turkish and Crusader ruins.

After a brief return to Damascus, we found that there was a train running almost daily from Damascus to Amman. At last we can go to Transjordan, and without any complications. No one told us not to go! We arrived rather late in the evening. Although Amman is a small town, there were two hotels. We, of course chose the cheaper one, but it was so infested with bedbugs we did not unpack our bags and moved out early in the morning, much to the astonishment of our host. We moved to the Philadelphia Hotel, which is twice as expensive and much nicer. It is a European hotel, not Arab. The concierge was surprised to see two American women so early in the morning; there was no

We inspect the hotel beds.

train due that day. For a long time there had been no American guests in Amman, but there were a few of other nationalities.

Transjordania is a country of Bedouins. People stared at us, because women hardly ever go on the streets, and never without veils. The police wouldn't let us go out unescorted. Amman is the capital of Transjordan. The country is ruled by the Amir Abdullah, an uncle of King Ghazi of Iraq, who was recently killed in an automobile accident. The Amir rules under British protection, like King Farouk of Egypt, but Transjordania is more independent than Egypt. The Arabs of Palestine and some of Transjordan dislike Amir Abdullah because he is in favor of cooperating with the British and partitioning Palestine. Nearly every man in the country carries a dagger, revolver, and an elephant tail whip. The Bedouins are fighters.

We spent the day exploring the hot desert town. Besides the two hotels, there were a few shops, mud huts and several modern stone houses. We visited all the Roman ruins left over from the time of the Ammorites. Our ability to appreciate old ruins is nearing the saturation point. As we scratched around in the dirt on one unexcavated mound, picking up shards of ancient pottery and iridescent glass, a wonderful peasant came by. He was armed with rifle, a belt of bullets across his chest, a dagger at his waist, and an elephant tail whip in hand. In spite of our obvious awe, he seemed quite friendly.

Our beds that night were luxurious, clean and white, and the running water in our room hot and sweet.

"Nance," said Gertrude, "Don't you think we have been on the road long enough?"

"Well, we have to be back at the end of this week."

"Why don't we just go back tomorrow and get a good rest before school starts?"

"It's only forty miles from here to Jerusalem, but how are we going to get there? There are no bus or train connections between Palestine and Transjordania."

"Mr. Azeeb said he thought the Allenby Bridge over the Jordan was closed."

"We've always found a way, so far. We'll find another."

The next morning, eating breakfast, we heard pistol shots. I complained to the manager. "We came here to get away from all the shooting in Palestine." He was most apologetic. It was just a couple of fellows testing out their new bullet-proof Buick. We found the men were British agents for an oil company and were planning to drive to Jerusalem that day. When they learned of our plight, they invited us to go with them. The bullets that they fired at the car made no dent, they did not even scratch the paint or crack the inch-thick glass. The steel doors were so heavy I couldn't pull them shut.

As we were starting off, another large car came by. It was Emir Abdullah returning from a gazelle hunt. The meeting of two cars in Amman is such a rare occurrence we had to stop and chat. Then, someone said, "Look, here comes His Highness, the son of the Emir." Naif Abdullah Hussein, the younger son of the royal ruler of Transjordania, had heard of our bullet-proof car and wanted to have a look at it. His lord high pasha opened the door and said in English, "His Highness would like to drive."

Our two oil agents got out, leaving me with the prince on the front seat and Gertrude with the pasha on the back seat. His English, being as feeble as my Arabic, the prince and I couldn't carry on a very weighty conversation, but it was fun driving through the town and having everybody salute as we passed. His Highness wanted to show us his military regiment and club outside of Amman. He drove like the wind, while the old pasha gently reminded him of "what happened to Your Royal Cousin, may Allah keep him." The prince of Persia recently had been killed in an automobile accident.

At Prince Hussein's club we had some exquisite lemonade. While the men talked, Gertrude and I sat on a red velvet couch, pulling down our skirts and trying discreetly not to cross our legs (an immodest American custom). Women in this country are not supposed to be intelligent enough to join in men's conversation. Every officer and servant who entered the room would pause on the threshold, click his heels, salute, then approach and kiss the prince's hand. Gertrude and I neglected this ritual, but later we made him teach us his special salute. His Highness invited us to come see his peacocks and his almond orchards. We threw flowers into his swimming pool and climbed the minaret of his private mosque. Gertrude said we were sorry we couldn't take pictures of his lovely place, and he immediately sent a servant to get a camera, which he begged us to keep for remembrance of him.

The bullet-proof car took us safely home through the hot valley of the Jordan and the Dead Sea. We could not open the windows for fear of de-bullet-proofing the car. The Allenby Bridge, the only one over the Jordan, was not closed. Our only disappointment was that nobody shot at us. Back in Ramallah, we found the gate to the school grounds locked. We climbed over the wall by way of a fig tree. Home again.

Love, Nance

The Amir should have bought the bullet-proof car. He was later assassinated while riding in his car.

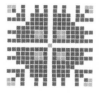

Spring, 1939

Journal Entry
May 23, 1939

    Gertrude and I are seriously considering the possibility of staying on another year. We are beginning to understand Arabic. We know the people and places, and I would like to have a second year of teaching here, now that I have gotten over the initial rough spots. Letters from our parents urge us to come home. I think they are tired of hearing about the dangers of life in Ramallah, but it is really easing up now. Living in danger and discomfort is not as bad as hearing about it. We hardly ever hear shooting any more. If, as it looks, there will really be a war in Europe, how would we get home?

May 27, 1939

    I have been working hard on a play, which my history classes are producing on Thursday. There has never been a dramatic production at Friends Girls School. This is just a series of scenes from European history that I wrote up the last three days of Spring vacation. The girls are excited about it, although they have no idea what a drama is. They have learned their lines, but feel very shy about saying them in public. The costumes we have concocted or borrowed from neighbors, and the girls are greatly concerned about whether one is prettier than another. Our most important character refused to wear the miter of Cardinal Richelieu until I threatened to play the part myself.

I have had help from our wonderful Wadia Shatarra, the most beloved of all the teachers. Wadia has been teaching at Friends Girls School for twenty-five years. Her stories, jokes, and wisdom have gotten all of us over many rough spots this year. Proud and patriotic, she understands the Arabs, "my people," and loves to teach us songs, or tell us stories about "Joha," the wise fool of Arabic folklore. Teacher of Arabic at both the Friends Schools, Widea, gives a children's radio hour once a week, heard all over Palestine.

Sit down with her some day and ask, "Widea, what happened to Ramallah during the world war?"

"Oh my, *habeebi*, those were terrible times."

"Were you teaching at this school then?"

"Teaching? My dear, could I come and teach British soldiers? *Yahbiyay*, these British took the schools for barracks. They used the study hall for a dormitory and drilled soldiers in the dining room."

"But Wadia, what happened to all the furniture?"

"*Harame*, those were terrible times. They burned the desks for fuel; they threw away the valuable pieces. We found the piano in a field near Ain Fara."

Our math teacher, lively Asma Ferris, keeps us informed on current events and never lets us forget the plight of the Arabs. She is deeply angry for her country and always dresses in black. Miss

Hannush, wise, firm and gentle, mothers us all. It is a delight to hear her laugh.

An important member of our school community, although she doesn't teach, is our neighbor, Nahmie Shahlah. Her vocation is to minister to the needy. Under the mulberry tree in Nahmie's courtyard, people come and sit. Nahmie feeds the poor and hungry, weeps with the sorrowing, scolds the wicked and naughty. Nahmie has a donkey who wakes the town every morning at 4:30 with loud and prolonged braying. The purpose of her donkey is to lend to neighbors who have no donkey. Nahmie has a vineyard where anyone may get grapes, or apricots from her trees. The whole town drinks from Nahmie's well. She is a pillar of the Friends meeting.

Although Nahmie wears western dress, her three quiet sisters wear the traditional Ramallah costume. They stay at home and care for their father, who has been ailing for many years. The morning he died we heard, not the donkey, but the sisters wailing and saw them tearing their gowns, right through the heavy frontal embroidery. The whole school rallied for the funeral, bringing food and running about the town to tell the news. G. and I were assigned the duty of making a funeral wreath from ivy and branches of juniper.

In his coffin of wood covered with velvet, Abu Shahlah looked very sweet, wearing his festival robes and best turban. As they brought him out into the courtyard everyone crowded around and shed loud tears. We all followed the procession through the streets, weeping and chanting, sloshing through puddles and over slippery stones. All the people ran out of their shops crying, "*Ma salame, Abu Shahlah!*" The church was so crowded I could not see much, but our wreath looked fine on the open coffin. Many beautiful tributes were paid to the Abu, for he had been a worthy father of his family and tribe. Only the oldest of his daughters was able to attend the funeral.

Afterwards, G. and I went back to the Shahlahs, where the

three younger daughters were sitting quietly weeping. The priest came in and all the women in the room stood up until he was seated. Ceremoniously he offered his condolences and then joined the tearful silence. Everyone says, "Poor girls, who will take care of them now?" But they have been taking care of Abu Shahlah for fifteen years. I guess they have lost their vocation.

On the third day after his death we heard an extra amount of noise going on in the Shahlah's courtyard. There were crowds of neighborhood people singing a strange chant while a circle of women in graceful Ramallah dress danced. Backward, forward, and sideways the women moved in a circle, with bouncy step, making pounding or whirling motions with their hands, their long, heavy shawls swinging from their heads. The family of the deceased sat on their balcony weeping in appreciation. For two weeks after the death, no one in the family must cook food. Women from Ramallah and neighboring villages came every day, carrying on their heads large bowls of rice, meat and bread, and from morning until night they danced for the bereaved.

The way to become really acquainted with Ramallah people is to ride on the bus to Jerusalem. This bus cannot run regularly because of strikes, curfews, sabotage, and permits. However, late in the winter it became fairly dependable. If you plan to go to Jerusalem, you must run out to the place where the bus starts and ask some loiterer when the bus will be going. He doesn't know, but he thinks it will be seven o'clock. You go at seven and find the bus left fifteen minutes ago. It was full, so it just left. The next day, go out at six-thirty and sit in the bus until it is full, around eight-thirty.

The passengers are a jolly, congenial group. They laugh and joke in Arabic and English. They help each other with bundles. If one doesn't have the three piasters fare, the driver will gladly give him credit until tomorrow. We do not discuss the weather, because the weather is so predictable in Palestine, but we talk politics, shouting our opinions from one end of the bus to another. We stop on the way at Bireh to take more people in the already-full bus. The children are placed on the laps of passengers; baskets and bundles in the aisles are used as seats. The next stop comes at a barricade across the road. British soldiers step into the bus, and all the men hold up their blue permits, which allow them to travel between towns. The soldiers are supposed to examine each one, but it is too difficult in such a stuffed bus. They wearily say, "Go on." After we have passed out of sight of the soldiers we stop and let on more passengers, those who have no permits.

The trip to Jerusalem is lovely. Passing a beautiful valley, I ask the woman next to me about it, because I love its story.

"What place is this, Khalti?" (One always addresses older women as Aunty.)

" It is Maaloofia. Over there on the hillside you see the robbers caves. On this side there is an ancient palace."

"But I see no palace."

"Of course not; it is buried under the hill."

"But how do you know it is there?"

"A few years ago some Americans dug it out and found the old castle. Now it is buried again."

"Buried again?"

"Of course. We need the land to cultivate more than we need the ruined castle."

We pass fields where peasants plow with oxen or camels yoked to wooden plows. Then there is a modern town, Callendia.

"What is this place Khalti?"

"Yahrubee. It is a Jewish colony. Five years ago this was a beautiful hill covered with olive trees. Now it is only a Jewish colony where airplanes land."

The hills are golden on the way to Jerusalem. We pass "Nebi Daoud," the hill of David, then a little town called Ain Fara, where we can see the low, white buildings of Jerusalem gleaming across the valley. Just before we come to the soldier's barricade, we stop behind a house and let out the passengers who have no permits. They finish the trip on foot through the unguarded roads. At Damascus gate the bus is met by a crowd of porters who climb up on the roof and throw down the baggage. These porters, dressed mostly in burlap bags and innumerable ropes and straps, are so strong that one man can carry a whole piano. I have seen it. The driver bids us goodbye and stands by his bus shouting *"el Ramallah!"* starting to collect passengers for his next busload back.

Porters

June 19, 1939

Dear Family,

Yesterday the American teachers hiked to Emmaus, with Nahmie and her donkey to guide us. Emmaus is the place where Jesus revealed his identity to the disciples after the Resurrection. It is about ten miles from Ramallah.

We started at 4:30 in the morning, the five of us and a Moslem fellow, Ibrahim, to protect us from the rebels. (He was a rebel leader, a friend of Nahmie's, nice fellow.) We took turns riding the donkey, but it is faster to walk. There were no roads, only paths. We met many peasants bringing their vegetables to the market in Ramallah. The women walk the ten or more miles to town, carrying baskets of fresh apricots or cucumbers on their heads. The men ride donkeys. Walking ahead of our group I met most of the peasants first. Of course they thought I was a Jew with my pale face and strange, foreign clothes. But when I spoke to them in my broken Arabic their faces changed, and they knew I was one of those Ramallah foreigners. They would stop and ask me where I was going. "May Allah give you feet that never tire."

Woman with cucumbers

We passed through villages that can only be reached by
footpath. We had to step aside to let the loaded camels pass. At
about 7:30 we came to the church that marks the spot where
Cleophas and his son, Simeon, received Jesus in their home. There
is a very beautiful picture of the breaking of the bread. A
Franciscan monk, an American, was delighted to show us around
and to speak his native language, after years of hearing only Italian
in his brotherhood. There is a German hospice at Emmaus, kept
by nuns. Around it are well-kept gardens and trees, almost a
woods, where we gloried in the shade and ate our lunch of
cucumbers, bread, and hardboiled eggs. The Franciscan monk
stayed with us, but refused to share our food. Nahmie tried,
unsuccessfully, to convert him to Quakerism.

For our last trip in Palestine, Kareemeh and Labeeb took us to
the Dead Sea. Jerusalem is about 1200 feet above sea level and The
Dead Sea 1200 feet below. The road winds down forty miles
through barren hills. Half way down we pass the ruined "Good
Samaritan Inn." Still farther down there is a small sign that says
SEA LEVEL, the only billboard in all of Palestine. Although they
tell us this is where David used to pasture his flocks, I can see
nothing for his sheep to eat. The hills are sharp and brown,
tossing ahead of us down to the blue Dead Sea, utterly parched.

At the Dead Sea there is a Jewish colony of salt miners and a
nice cool hotel where we had lunch and changed to our bathing
suits. Outside the hotel, heat rises in wavering streaks from
everything. We had to hop on the hot pebbles to keep from
getting burned. There is no basking in the sun by the Dead Sea;
you must plunge into the warm brine, a thick, resisting liquid in
which you cannot swim. It is like pushing against heavy doors.
Wading out to the deep water, your feet are lifted under you,
giving an uncomfortable sensation that something is trying to
turn you upside down. You stretch luxuriously and lie for an hour
in the deep water. If you splash, the stinging brine gets into your

eyes and nose. You can take a book (Labeeb smoked a cigarette), but wear a hat to keep off the beating rays of the sun. Coming out, you are slippery with brine. Take a shower and wash out your bathing suit, or it will be in holes the next time you put it on.

Coming up from the Dead Sea, we told Kareemeh and Labeeb we would be leaving Palestine when school closed for the summer. They seemed hurt, as if it were their fault we are going back to America. With war brewing in Europe, there is no question of our staying on. We have made arrangements to travel by Greek freighter to Italy, meet my sister, Mary, in Rome, and go through Switzerland to Germany, where I will attend yearly meeting at Bad Pyrmont and Gertrude will go with Mary to France. I will meet them in Paris for a fling before dashing over to London and taking a nice respectable ship of the Cunard White Star Line to New York on August 29, 1939.

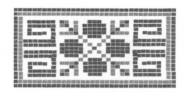

The Long Way Home

August 1939

It didn't quite work out that way. On the morning of July 10, we waited at the port of Tel Aviv, with Labeeb and Kareemeh to see us off.

"Where is the boat?"

"Out there."

There is no Pier at Tel Aviv. The *S.S. Attika* was moored a few miles off the coast. In a small tender-boat we were taken out to the big freighter, watched the sailors take our precious trunks up a rickety ladder and then, after waiting for a convenient wave, leaped to the ladder ourselves, while the big boat rocked and the little boat tossed. The trunks were to go sealed "in bond" to New York, so that we would not have to bother with them as we traveled in Europe. But they sat for a week on the deck of the *Attika*, splashed and salted by the Mediterranean. We wondered how our treasures, our Damascus brasses, our Oriental rugs, our Ramallah embroideries and inlaid boxes, carved trinkets, were faring. We were the only passengers to board at Tel Aviv.

The Washing Trough on SS Attika

The freighter was filthy. Deep in the hold was a small dormitory for third-class passengers; the best of the bare canvas bunks had already been taken by passengers who boarded at Jaffa. Next to my bunk slept an Italian nun, and I thought, "Aha, now I will find out what a nun wears under her habit." Alas, throughout the whole voyage, melting heat, cold, storm and seasickness, she never once removed her clothes, or even her veil. She kept spotlessly clean. As we were getting settled, Gertrude, who has always been neat, said, "Where shall I hang my clothes?"

"Shall I call your maid, Madamoiselle? She could hang your gowns on the pipes overhead and put your cold cream in the seasick box."

A funny little man came lurching between the bunks. Grinning and bowing to us, he made a long speech in Greek. We grinned and bowed and said, "Thank you." To Gertrude I said, "Who was that? One of your admirers?"

"Why I never saw the man before; I thought he was yours."

Turned out he was the steward, Lazaret. We found we had one word of vocabulary in common with Lazaret, "mangez." Food was served on a wooden plank in the dormitory, but it was several days before G. and I could work up an appetite for that greasy and unsanitary mess. Our friends had given us cookies and fruit. To escape the seasick stench downstairs, we slept on the deck, on bales of Egyptian cotton, but after the men in third class discovered how comfortable the cotton bales were, we slept on sacks of potatoes taken on board at Cyprus. Our coats served as blankets. When it grew very cold at night, or when we were splashed by waves, we warmed up in the engine room. For washing there was a sort of trough, cold water, of course, and the toilet was so unspeakable that G. and I covertly used the Captain's latrine while he was dining. In the daytime, passengers from first and second class came down to join our parties on the cotton bales. We sang, talked, and had our portraits drawn by a Syrian artist.

For a whole day, we anchored off shore at Famagusta on the Island of Cyprus, to load potatoes — winches squeaking all night, hot sun all day. The captain allowed us to go ashore to bicycle around the town. There are three hundred and sixty five churches in Famagusta, a famous old Roman fort, used by crusaders, improved by Turks, and taken by the British. In the port were four British battleships and an Italian passenger ship. The Island of Cyprus is beautiful with its rugged and misty mountains. If the Greeks cannot hold it, the British will grab it to keep it from the Italians. At Larnica, more potatoes were brought from shore in small boats, hours and hours. The Captain let down the ladder so that we could swim in the deep waters off shore but before long he had the boat whistle blown and he signaled for us to come aboard. It seems they had sighted sharks around us. Tantalizing, it was to sail past the mountains of Turkey and the Island of Rhodes without stopping, but we were way off schedule.

The Mountains of Turkey
From the deck of S.S. Attika
Passenger sits on Cargo of Potatoes
July 1939

Landing at Piraeus, we found our boat was twelve hours late and had missed the connecting boat we were supposed to take from Athens to Brindisi. Nevertheless, Greek lines had to put us up over night in an Athens hotel and provide train tickets across Greece where we could catch the boat to Brindisi. Two Greek men whom we had met took us to dinner and then up to see the Acropolis by moonlight with the Parthenon gleaming in majestic beauty, perhaps the best way to see it, but we were disappointed not to see it by day. Our train left too early in the morning.

The boat from Athens to Brindisi could not take its usual route through the Corinthian Canal because the walls of the canal had fallen just a few days before. Going around the Pelopenesian Peninsula had delayed the boat just enough so that, crossing Greece by train, we could catch it on the western shore of Greece. It was an overnight sail to Brindisi, a night we spent on deck chairs on first class and dancing with the Greek ship's officers.

August and September 1939

At the hotel in Brindisi we scrubbed and splashed in the hot running water. The clean sheets of the beds smelled sweet, and for the first time in a week we slept in pajamas instead of fully clothed. Laundry was draped all around the room, where we slept peacefully on our soft beds.

In the morning, we rushed to the Cunard White Line to see if they couldn't ship our trunks to Paris where we would pick them up when we sailed. For an hour we argued. The agency had never shipped trunks before. Finally, we persuaded them that this was part of our due along with our steamship tickets and left the trunks in their gracious care, hoping to find them in Paris. They absolutely would not ship Gertrude's crated copper table and extra suitcase. We must send them from Rome, they said.

So, we boarded the train for Rome with three suitcases, a crated table, and my *"falaheen"* bundle like Palestinian peasants carry while traveling. (It was my reversible raincoat rolled up with extra sweater, shoes, and slacks that would not fit in my suitcase. These were held together with a patent rubber handle that Mother had given me before I left home.)

The trip from Brindisi to Rome takes a whole, hot day. But the green trees and hills of Italy were sweet to eyes that had looked so long on the brown mountains of Palestine. Although third class on the train was crowded, we thought it luxurious after Oriental trains. Some Italians bought us bottles of "mineral water," a thick, bitter water, which is almost worse than being thirsty.

That day we crossed the Appenine Mountains and passed back of our old friend Vesuvius. In Naples we changed to the Rome

Express, such a luxurious train that Gertrude and I couldn't believe our upholstered coach was meant for third-class passengers. It must be the doing of Mussolini, we said. However, when the conductor came to collect our tickets I could not help feeling a little guilty as I handed him the pink third-class billet. He made no remarks and left us alone staring at each other.

A nice, young Italian joined us in our compartment. He could not speak English, but we got along in French. He explained all the glories of the Fascist government. Once in a while I would condescendingly translate a bit of our conversation to Gertrude. By the time we reached Rome, I was almost a Fascist and an admirer of Mussolini, but I forgot all about politics in the excitement of seeing Mary.

Mary says she will never get over the shock of her first sight of me after a year's absence. Walking through the streets of Rome, I was carrying Gertrude's crated table on my head and the "falaheen" bundle on my arm. The table was too heavy to carry any other way. Gertrude looked more civilized, with only two large suitcases.

Mary had been traveling for a month in France and Italy. We lay awake half the night checking up on our adventures. Mary felt much fresher than we did, for she had not been traveling steerage.

Rome was beautiful. Gertrude and I could not get accustomed to the bright, modern shops, the stylish people. We visited all the places one should see in Rome and Florence. Such a whirl of beautiful and historical things to see in one week that we could only go gasping in the trail of Mary, who is a knowledgeable guide to the wonders of Italian art and folk lore.

One restful afternoon we spent sleeping on the top of the tower of Pisa, several sunny mornings tramping the dignified streets of Florence — drifting into medieval days in the Medici palace, worshipping with Fra Angelico over his exquisite Madonnas in San Marco, and trying vainly to appreciate the crowded masterpieces in the Uffizzi Gallery. It was like listening to several great symphonies at once.

Evenings we spent at public concerts in the town square, walking home past a delicatessen shop where Gertrude insisted on buying candied bananas, Mary on petting the six-toed cat, and I on consuming watery imitations of American ice cream sodas.

From Florence we sped on to the magic of Venice. People go to Venice to see if it is true the streets are made of water. It is true, as are the arched foot bridges, the black gondolas, the gay piazza de San Marco, and St. Mark's itself, a jewel of Byzantine architecture inlaid with gold mosaics. Better than viewing the cathedrals, I loved to wander through streets and become part of a city, to buy Italian bread and cheese and munch it sitting on a bridge, and at night to dine on a plate of the clear soup, patina, generously laden with thin spaghetti and sprinkled with powdered cheese.

After Venice we separated. Since Mary had already been to Switzerland, we left her to wander through the Tyrol and meet us again in Salzburg. Gertrude and I took a train through the Simplon Pass to Switzerland, stopping for the night in the little town of Visp at the foot of the Alps.

A cog rail carries travelers five thousand feet up from Visp to Zermatt at the foot of the Matterhorn. I can never forget that lovely day. As the train climbed up and up, new snow-clad peaks leaped into view: green slopes all around us and the high, high mountaintops gleaming golden in the morning sun.

We established ourselves in Zermatt at the Pension Alpenblick, a clean, white inn on the outskirts of the town. That day Gertrude and I took fresh bread and cheese and climbed five thousand feet more to the Gorner Grat, one of the lesser peaks of Switzerland. Its woody trail below the timberline and its rocky slopes above gave us a good taste of Alpine climbing.

The most delicious meal I have ever eaten was that bread and cheese on the Gornegrat. The sweetest night's sleep I have known was that night in the tingling mountain air when, worn from the day's climb, I crawled into a white feather bed and slept, hearing the rushing mountain stream all night long. How glorious to rise in the morning and look out of the window at the towering Matterhorn!

We spent another day in Zermatt, explored the colorful shops, slept in a green mountain meadow, and I climbed alone half way up another mountain at sunset and sat looking long at the glacial majesty of the Alps.

We were sorry indeed to leave Zermatt and spent a long day on the train going from Brig through Lucerne, with only some hard black bread for lunch. We spent the night in Zürich. What an odd night it was. We persuaded a woman in an apartment house to make up a room for us. I sat on the balcony half the night drying my hair, and the next day we carried our bags a long way through the park, and across a beautiful bridge to the station. Zürich is a clean city, like all of Switzerland.

We took a streamlined ferry across Lake Constance into Germany and spent the rest of our Swiss money for a delicious breakfast. In Münich Gertrude and I parted for the first time in a year. She went to see about a job she had heard of — teaching in a German school for girls. I went on to Salzburg and met Mary in a youth hostel. The next day we went to Vienna, a long train trip along the Danube. German trains are even more crowded than those in the Orient. There were a great many Nazi soldiers who wanted to argue with us about politics. I expressed my views freely, criticizing the Nazi regime, and the soldiers were delighted to show me how wrong I was.

The city is too clean since Hitler reorganized it. The streets are wide, and the old Hapsburg buildings still sit in majestic splendor. We strolled in the gardens of Maria Theresa's palace. In the evening we went riding on a Ferris wheel.

Trains here are really more interesting than cities, because

Europe is so small that when people travel on trains they think they are going a tremendous distance. They practically set up housekeeping in a compartment. One woman spent fifty miles getting dinner for her children. She had brought with her a jar of milk, several paper bags containing bread, cereal, salt, sugar, lettuce and fruit, and a basket of utensils. These she spread out on the seat amid much jolting of the train. Then she mixed up a dish of milk and cereal with flavoring, cut up the bread, made salads of meat and lettuce, and peeled the fruit for the children.

It was a regular Thanksgiving dinner, and by the time she reached her destination, a great deal of the meal was spread over the seat and over her fellow passengers. She tied the remaining lettuce and butter in a bag, which she hung out of the train window to keep cool. We gratefully handed the equipment out to her after she had herded the children out of the train.

Gertrude had landed the job in Munich and was going to stay in Europe. I left Mary and her sitting wistfully on a station platform, and I went alone to attend the Friends yearly meeting in Bad Pyrmont, to which I had been appointed as a delegate by my Quaker meeting in Baltimore. I would see Mary again in Paris, but Gertrude — who knows when we would meet again!

I spent a miserable night changing trains five times, trying to sleep in trains and stations. In Berlin I was awed, watching the soldiers march in goose-step. But when I failed to give the Nazi salute, they hissed. Pretty creepy, that.

At the Friends Yearly Meeting in Bad Pyrmont, the talk was guarded; we all knew that there were Gestapo present. One courageous English woman, Mary Fredrich, who was married to a German, Hans Fredrich, invited a few of us foreigners to her home for tea. It was there, behind closed doors and shuttered windows, that I learned the plight of the Jews. The restrictions, the shame, the persecution. Many are not allowed to go out of their homes; Mary Fredrich took food to them.

After the conference, I went hiking for three days with a group of young German Friends, mostly professional people and foreign Quakers. Deep in the Black Forest our leader, Hans Fredrich, encouraged them to talk, and I learned it was not only the Jews who suffered under the grinding heel of the Nazi regime.

As we tramped along the dusty roads, we sang lustily, stopped on high hilltops to sleep in a meadow and talk, and camped overnight at youth hostels. We pushed on through drenching rain until my shoes wore out, and we had to stop and repair them. Henri, the French lad, suggested that I get sabots (wooden shoes). The German boys, frugal ones, repaired the shoes with rope. Our fellowship was close, for we all feared that before another month passed our countries would be at war with one another. It made our friendship all the dearer to us.

After leaving the group, I took a night train for Paris. Stopping for a few hours in Cologne, I spent the rest of my German money, for one can't take it out of Germany or change it into any other money. The train ran all night from Cologne to Paris. There were only two others in my compartment — a German youth, who spoke neither French nor English, and René, a French doctor. We decided to get some real sleep. The German lad stretched out on one bench, I on the other, and Rene on the floor between us.

We bought candy and shared it. In spite of our plans for sleep, René and I talked most of the night on the philosophy of war, of science, of France, and men and women. Neither of us could speak German, but we were friendly with the boy and joked with him in perfect understanding, as people can do even when they do not speak the same tongue. The uneasy German lad was obviously escaping from Nazi Germany.

At the border, I had some trouble. The date on my French visa was marked "before July 10." This was August 9, and the passport official said my visa was invalid. He spoke only French, and my explanations and prayers in feeble French were inadequate. He took my baggage off the train along with the passport, said I must wait on the station platform 'til morning and then see some officials. It was midnight then. The station was closed, and I would only have to wait nine or ten hours sitting beside the heavy, barbed wire and dynamite barricade that marked the border between France and Germany in August 1939.

The train was ready to pull out. Even René's long arguments were unavailing to the passport official. But I had a sudden inspiration. In French I said:

"But, *Monsieur*, I must go to Paris. I will miss the boat sailing for America tomorrow."

"Eh? You are sailing for America tomorrow?"

"Yes," I lied. The date of my sailing was two weeks hence.

"Let me see your steamship ticket."

I produced the ticket, trembling. The official turned it around several times. He could not read the ticket, which was printed in English.

"Very well," he said. "You must not miss the boat. You may go without a visa."

In Paris, Mary was waiting at the American Express. She was to sail on the *Mauretania* on August 11. We had one day together in Paris. I tried to change my passage to her boat, but the *Mauretania* was all booked up. I would sail two weeks later on the *Aquitania*. I went down to Le Havre to see Mary off when the *Mauretania* pulled out of harbor at 2 a.m.

I was utterly alone. There was no room for me in the dingy hotel across from the station, but the janitor let me sit in a squeaky wicker chair while he mopped up the floors of the café. At 5 a.m. I slipped out, giving the janitor a two-franc piece, and I took the train for Rouen. Weary as I was from lack of sleep, I roamed through the lacy cathedrals of Rouen and in the old Norman tower where Jeanne d'Arc had spent her last days, I curled up in the empty fireplace and slept.

Back in Paris, I went often to visit Notre Dame and was captivated by its timeless charm, as so many have been before me. Paris is not a city for an innocent girl to wander alone. Often men would follow me. *"Vous êtes jolie, Mademoiselle; ou allez-vous?"* I dodged into hotels, shops, and museums.

One day on the top of the Arc de Triomphe, I sat a long time looking at Paris. A French man kept annoying me, asking how I liked Paris, trying to make a date. Fortunately he spoke no English. When he asked what I was doing that afternoon, I said I was going out with my brother.

"Vôtre frère? Mais, où est-il?"

I looked around. There was an American boy sitting on the railing. I could tell that he was American by his casual slacks and jacket, his saddle shoes, and the way he held his cigarette.

"That's my brother," I told the Frenchman.

He would not believe me and persisted in following me until I went up to the American boy and said in desperation, "Do you mind being my brother for a few minutes until I get rid of this pest? I told him you were my brother."

The American boy grinned. He spoke in a heavenly southern accent.

"Sure, I'll be your brother any time you want."

The flabbergasted Frenchman retreated in defeat. My brother was one of those poverty-stricken American students newly arrived in Paris. That night he took me out to dinner and insisted on ordering champagne even though I never did like champagne. We spent half the night laughing and throwing stones into the Seine from the Notre Dame bridge.

I made other friends in Paris. Mr. Thurlow came to my rescue while I was arguing with the stationmaster at the *Gare de Lyon*. I was trying to get him to send my trunk on the Cherbourg to meet the *Aquitania*. The stationmaster thought I should open it for inspection and pay customs. He stood with a knife ready to break the seal that held it in bond. I grabbed his arm and shouted in French: "No, no, it must not be broken until I reach America!"

Then Mr. Thurlow came and helped me out. Somehow he persuaded the officials to send my trunk, still bonded, down to Cherbourg and there to put it on the *Aquitania* for me. Bless your heart, Mr. Thurlow. He was a middle-aged man, a French teacher from Detroit, having a good time in Europe. He was delighted to find a companionable girl and insisted on showing me the nightlife of Paris.

Another day I stood puzzling over the direction map in the Metro. A young man was puzzling over the same map, and we were soon trying to explain it to each other in halting French.

"My gosh, do you know any English?" the young man asked.

He was another lost American, and artist and writer. He took me to dinner and to the Louvre (where much of the art was stored underground in anticipation of war). We also wandered along the banks of the Siene, browsing over the second-hand books and envying the lazy *"Clochards,"* the tramps who sleep and fish all day under the bridges.

I decided to spend my last week in England. I persuaded the Cunard White Star line that my steamship ticket entitled me to a free trip from Paris to London, then crossed by way of Boulogne, Folkstone, and landed in London at midnight with no English money. A kind man gave me a six pence, which I spent on the bus.

I was looking for the youth hostel on Great Ormand Street. Someone told me to get off at Southampton Row and walk through some dingy alleys until I found it. My two suitcases were heavy. Dozens of men followed me, wanting to show me the way. One tall fellow stepped beside me and said, "Don't listen to them, Miss. Those are dangerous fellows. I'm the Chief of Police in this district, and I'll take care of you."

He did not look like any Chief of Police I'd ever seen in his black, civilian suit and with no hat. I stepped into a hotel doorway and set down the heavy suitcase for a moment, weak with fear and weariness. The tall man went over and spoke a few low words to the clerk. While his back was turned, I stepped out and hurried on through the midnight streets. Several more young men wanted to help me out. Finally I picked one whom I felt was a good and honest man. Really, intuition is a marvelous thing. He carried my heaviest suitcase to the youth hostel and rang the bell. It was now half past midnight, an hour when inmates are not admitted to youth hostels. Seeing my predicament, however, the warden let me in and gave me a bunk.

London is the most dignified and mellow city of the world. I loved its stiff buildings of brick and stone, the towering omnibuses, houses of Parliament, and memory-crowded Westminster Abbey. John, a friend I had met in Germany, took me on a very sooty steamboat excursion up the Thames to Kew Gardens. (When Thames' boats go under low bridges, they have a patented method of collapsing the smokestack and blasting all the soot back in the faces of passengers.)

Wanting to see some English countryside, I hired a bicycle and planned a short hostelling trip through Devon. A Canadian youth staying at the Central London Youth Hostel decided to accompany me. Russell was very patient with my inexperienced cycling. Indeed, I would never have gotten through without him, for he stopped and fixed things whenever my bicycle broke down. He picked me up when I forgot to go on the left side and ran into an automobile.

We stopped often to rest on the sunny hillsides or explore quaint, old graveyards. In the evenings, we swapped yarns and folk songs with other youth hostelers around roaring fires in ancient farm houses.

At last it was August twenty-third, the day I was to turn my face to America once more. I took the special boat train to Southampton feeling sad and happy. The London I left was preparing for war, digging trenches in Hyde Park, dragging heavy cables from balloons high over the city to prevent sudden air raids. I wanted to stay and see it through with the people of London.

The *Aquitania* was clumsy, a four-stack boat.

"This is her twenty-sixth year on the Atlantic," the first mate told me, "and probably her last trip over."

We were only half way across when the war broke out in Europe. Germany marched into Poland, but the passengers were not informed of it. Immediately all our portholes and windows were painted black.

"It's a blackout," we whispered excitedly to one another. "What has happened?"

I cabled Mother and Dad to meet me in New York, but there was no answer. No radio communication was going out from the ship. I thought, "We are isolated in this little shipboard world, tossing about on the Atlantic Ocean. What HAS happened out there?"

One night during a storm, I spent half the night up on the deck of the bow getting drenched by every exciting wave that broke over her. When the sea and wind grew so rough that I had to hold on with both hands to keep from being tossed overboard, my common sense got the better of the spirit of adventure.

"Really," I thought, "it would be a pity for me to be drowned now, when I'm almost home."

In the cold, rainy dawn of September first, we spotted the low shore of Long Island.

"It's America!" I said, jumping up and down and hitting my friend, Harry, on the back.

"Sure," said Harry, "that's what they call it."

Four hours later we idled past the Statue of Liberty. Harry wondered at my excitement. "Isn't it the same as when you left it a year ago?"

I could not tell him how different it was. How could I tell anyone what I knew of this good America, or of the haunting broadness of the earth, and a wistful restlessness, the East wind fever that was always to conflict with the dearness of home?

Epilogue

Returning from the adventurous year in Palestine to teach in a quiet, Quaker school in Maine, was a culture shock. In my spare time, I organized the letters my family had saved, and, for fun, made drawings to go with them. Then I put them away for about fifty years.

Nostalgic for more excitement, the next year I took a job as assistant director of the International Student House in Washington, D.C. Foreigners were flocking into the Capitol city — some of them refugees, all of them needing something. Our country was deciding whether to get into the war in Europe; Eleanor Roosevelt, turning up wherever morale was low, sometimes appeared at the International House to cheer the foreign students. She was a wonder.

It was there I met my future husband, James McDowell, who was working for the government before getting his Ph.D. After we married, I carried Palestine with me into Indiana, probably boring people, and even made it into stories for my children. At Earlham College, where Jim taught psychology, there were a few people who had studied or worked in the Middle East. Their accounts of the continuing hardships of the Palestinian Arabs have provided a

sobering balance to my rich and busy life in the Earlham
community and my family. Newspaper reports of events in foreign
countries, pictures of their leaders shaking hands with our
President have not moved me. My empathy is with the ordinary
people, not only Arabs but Bosnians, Africans, and all the folks
who are pushed out and bombarded from their homes.

After fifty years, I was able to see Gertrude again. She, too, has
had a full life, a charming family, and a yen to travel. She is the
same bubbling personality that I knew in 1938 and 1939.

Jim and I have hiked in many of the mountain ranges in
Europe and America, thankful that there is still wilderness in the
world and people who care. The substance of my life these eighty-
five years has not been "Who am I?" and "Where am I going?" No,
it is delight in a sense of becoming and belonging in this
unknowable cosmos. I quote to myself the line from Tennyson's
Ulysses:

"I am a part of all that I have met."

*Students at Ramallah Friends Girls School
with Kareemeh Nasser, teacher*

About the Author

Nancy Parker McDowell is a graduate
of Earlham School of Religion. She is
still an adventurer, who makes her
home in Richmond, Indiana.